A Year to Change
Your Mind

Dr Lucy Maddox is a consultant clinical psychologist with many years' experience of working in mental health, mostly in NHS and charity settings. She is also an experienced lecturer, writer and podcaster, and has written for publications including the *Guardian*, *The Times* and *Prospect* magazine. Her previous books are *Blueprint: How Our Childhood Makes Us Who We Are* (for adults) and *What is Mental Health?* (for children aged 10+).

A Year to Change Your Mind

Ideas from the Therapy Room to Help You Live Better

DR LUCY MADDOX

ALLEN&UNWIN

Published in hardback in Great Britain in 2022 by Allen & Unwin,
an imprint of Atlantic Books Ltd.

Illustrations by Tim Ruffle

10 9 8 7 6 5 4 3 2 1

A CIP catalogue record for this book is available from
the British Library.

Hardback ISBN: 978 1 83895 909 8
Trade paperback ISBN: 978 1 83895 628 8
E-book ISBN: 978 1 83895 629 5

Printed and bound by CPI Group (UK) Ltd, Croydon CR0 4YY

Allen & Unwin
An imprint of Atlantic Books Ltd
Ormond House
26–27 Boswell Street
London
WC1N 3JZ

www.allenandunwin.com/uk

Contents

Introduction

The way we think, experience the world and the other people in it, how we make decisions – it's all psychology. When things go wrong and we feel bad, or when our experiences tip into feeling *so* bad that they match the criteria for mental illness and severe distress, then clinical psychology and psychotherapy ideas can help. But we don't have to be at rock bottom to benefit from tried and tested concepts from the field of psychology. Many of those same principles can be useful for coping with universal human experiences that are less distressing, but can still trouble us. We can use them every day to enable us to make the most of life.

Using psychological insights to try to make things the best they can be is a rich area of research and practice: over time, psychologists have turned to the study of optimal functioning as well as thinking about how to address difficulties. The American psychologist Martin Seligman had a lot to do with the shift towards positive psychology from the late nineties onwards, when he called for a change from only thinking about problems, to instead investigating how best to build on strengths. The roots of the positive psychology movement go even further back, though, including the work of people like Carl Rogers, who saw everyone as having the potential to become the best they can be.

The spectrum of human experience is just that, a spectrum, and many symptoms of mental illness are increasingly seen as one end of a range of experience which we all exist along. This isn't to downplay the severity of mental illness: feeling a bit blue is different from feeling depressed, and having some tendencies towards worry is different from full-blown anxiety. But some of the approaches used in therapy for specific problems can be helpful in our everyday lives, and I often think that ideas I've shared in a therapy session are helpful outside a therapy context too. I use many of them myself.

I started training as a clinical psychologist when I was twenty-four. Looking back now, that seems young, but I didn't feel that young at the time. I came to the course, at University College London in Bloomsbury, from a year spent working as a research assistant into bipolar disorder in Camberwell, South London. Before that I'd studied for a master's in neuroscience, at the Institute of Psychiatry which was also in Camberwell, whilst at the same time juggling several other jobs to survive the brutal reality of expensive London life. I worked at the Science Museum as an explainer on Saturdays and I tutored psychology A level in the evenings. Before that I'd spent a year in Paris teaching English, and before that I'd studied an undergraduate degree in psychology, philosophy and physiology at Oxford University. I hadn't known that I would apply for clinical psychology training when I first started studying, but the bits I kept enjoying the most about the different jobs and courses all had to do with people, and clinical psychology sounded like a way of combining the science of psychology with a way to practically help others.

Clinical psychology training is a hybrid of three main elements: being taught about the principles and practical skills of therapy, conducting a research project into some area of mental health and spending time on placement in the National Health Service. The placements are in a range of areas, across the lifespan, and they include working with children, adults, older adults, people with learning disabilities and a couple of specialist placements which you can choose. I chose a placement in sexual health and a placement in an adolescent mental health ward, and I felt so drawn to working in the ward setting with teenagers that I wrote off emails to lots of wards in London asking if they had any jobs coming up. There was something about the intensity of the work which I found almost addictive: the potential for a great deal of change, at a time which is often a crisis, the huge amount that psychology can bring to that setting, and also the connection I felt I had with the teenagers. Luckily for me, South London and Maudsley NHS Trust did have a job coming up, and I worked with this Trust for eight years after qualifying, learning so much from some amazing colleagues as well as the young people there, before moving on to a different Trust to take up a consultant clinical psychologist position on a different ward. I left ward work in 2017, and worked in a mix of charity roles as consultant clinical psychologist for Action for Children, and as Senior Clinical Advisor for the British Association for Behavioural and Cognitive

Psychotherapies. Alongside this, I took on a small amount of private practice both with young people and adults, and I also studied for another master's, this time in organizational psychology, as my interest in how to improve workplaces and healthcare services grew. Then, in 2022, I moved to take up a research fellowship at the University of Bath, one which allows me to return to the NHS very part-time as a clinician too, and which combines my interest in psychology both for individuals and organizations (with my research context being back in inpatient wards for teenagers again).

Alongside my clinical roles I've enjoyed juggling a few other things, including lecturing and a great love of sharing ideas from psychology, in writing and audio. I published *Blueprint*, about how our childhood influences us, in 2018, and a book for children, *What is Mental Health?*, in 2020. I've been mulling over the idea for this book for a little while now, wanting to examine what I think are some of the most useful concepts that I've learnt through my training and practice as a clinical psychologist. Things that anyone can pick up. Sometimes I've chosen these ideas because I've personally found them useful in my own life as well as using them to help other people, and sometimes they're ideas which through the years I have found I return to again and again with the people who have come to see me for therapy. They're not random concepts, they're rooted in research evidence and based on theories about why they should be helpful. A lot of them are from cognitive behavioural therapy, but there are also some other approaches woven in, including narrative therapy, solution-focused therapy and family therapy. I've tried to be clear about which type of therapy I'm talking about, in case you want to go away and find out more.

Psychology underpins our whole lives. It is involved in our relationships, the places we live and work, and the dilemmas, large and small, which we encounter daily. This book draws on principles from psychological therapies to help us with the human experiences we all face. A calendar year gives us the chance to feel through all the different moods of the seasons and the patterns they might tempt us to fall into, some of them less helpful than others. A year is also a chance to remember previous years, including all their landmarks of memory, both joyful and painful, and to plan for our future selves. It's human to face similar dilemmas again and again. Falling into cyclical behaviours that we're not happy about doesn't always mean we've returned to square one, it means we're still learning and practising, and living a thoughtful life. It would be much worse not to notice the cycles we're part of.

I've used the year's cycle as a framework to explore those themes and ideas which I have found frequently come up in therapy sessions. The book chapters go month by month, from January to December, considering what is going on at this time of year and which ideas from psychological therapy might be particularly helpful to consider in that particular month. It includes psychology experiments, ideas from clinical practice and musings on real-life dilemmas. Of course, the dilemmas presented in each month don't belong solely to that time of year, and hopefully the ideas for how to help will be useful at any time.

January starts with New Year resolutions. New Year has a lot to answer for. On one arbitrary date we're all invited to review our lives and choose to make big or small changes to ourselves or what we're doing. In this chapter I think about how ideas from psychology and psychological therapy can help us with decisions, with making changes and with sticking to changes once we've decided on them.

February is a dark month in the northern hemisphere, and can seem to stretch on forever. Wherever we are in the world, the tone of this month can feel dark too, as we often realize that we've abandoned many of the promises to ourselves that we made in January. It's easy to feel stuck at this time of year. Sometimes it can be hard to motivate ourselves to move forward towards a goal, even when we know it's what we want. There's a lot we can learn from treatments for some clinical problems which can help us day to day with this stuck feeling. One key idea is that our actions, even small ones, can change how we feel – this is a powerful tool to have in our repertoire.

March can be a time to think about how to make the places and spaces we inhabit better for us. Spring is traditionally a season for clearing out and decluttering. This chapter considers what we *really* know about how the environments where we spend our time can influence our health, and how we can use these ideas to improve ours. From studies in hospitals which harness the power of nature to improve healing, to the effect of urban environments on stress, there is good evidence that our surroundings matter both psychologically and physically.

The objects in our home or office also matter, and I look at studies on hoarding disorder and talk about how to let go of things we don't need.

In April, as things are growing around us, we think about how to talk to ourselves in a way which encourages us to bloom too. We spend a lot of time in our own company, and if our inner voice is often having a go then it's going to have a negative effect. Learning to spot how we are speaking to ourselves, and taking steps to do something about it, can reap big rewards.

In May, the start of summer is almost here, and this season of lightness might encourage us to face outwards more than in. This chapter highlights what psychology can teach us about the art of talking... and listening. During my training I remember feeling tied up in conversational knots in the pub as a side effect of weeks spent analysing what we said and how we said it, yet a lot of techniques from therapy can be useful for other conversations in life too. This chapter also covers assertiveness and how to have a constructive row.

In June the longer evenings stretch ahead and give us more time and often more energy to relate to the people around us. Festivals, parties, holidays, weddings... these all present the opportunity to let loose a bit more. Sometimes, though, it can be hard to feel properly connected to others. Things can get in the way. In particular, in this chapter we consider the obstacles of social anxiety, the shadow of previously unhelpful relationships and the possibility of misunderstanding each other.

In July the likelihood of heatwaves might amplify any existential dread that we may be prone to. We've all had plenty of existential threats in the last few years: climate emergency, pandemic, on top of the usual existential dread which can appear for no reason at three in the morning. This chapter focuses on how psychology studies about climate change, Covid-19 and managing uncertainty in general can help us. Just what is useful when we are experiencing existential panic about a real existential problem?

In August, the height of summer seems like a good time to talk about anger. Studies show there's a potential downside of hot weather: increased anger and irritability. Why do we get grumpy in the heat and how can we avoid lashing out? In particular, psychology offers us some helpful ideas about how to regulate big emotions.

September reminds me of going back to school as a child: I always had a mix of fear and excitement before the new term began. As an adult many people tend to have some dread about work all year round. That Sunday night feeling that the fun is over and that we're back on the treadmill in the morning can prompt heartsink. We spend so much time at work that a lot of our dilemmas are based there too. This chapter considers how we can craft our jobs to be better for us, in several different ways.

In October, the falling leaves and drawing in of the nights can leave us feeling that we are entering a darker time. Winter happens every year, but the change and the loss it brings can still feel bleak. It makes me think of other cycles of loss we experience throughout our lives. We will all be touched by loss in one way or another, whether that's the ending of a relationship, the loss of people we love through bereavement, or other losses which might be couched as more 'minor' but which can loom just as large. This chapter reflects upon what can help us to cope with loss, why we can sometimes be extra-sensitive to it, and how we can hold ourselves kindly in the face of grief.

In November it's easy to feel tired. Days are short, and the lessening of the light can impact on our mood and make us want to hibernate. That's not necessarily a bad thing. This chapter considers why rest is so important, what we can do about it and how we can try to improve our sleep. There's a lot to juggle in life, and we're probably all working hard in one way or another. Ultimately rest is as important as action: it might help to see it as an action in itself.

Finally, December's chapter encourages us to think about negotiating family and managing expectations. December can be a tricky time: relatives packed together at close quarters isn't always a recipe for happiness and harmony. Why are family relationships thrown into relief at Christmas and how can we get through it? How can we use radical acceptance to cope with our Christmas reality? And how can we shift away from unhelpful behaviours which don't serve us well?

In the epilogue I pull all these chapters together, and consider how the year's cycle is just one of the many cycles we all experience as we live our lives. The year provides us with some helpful anchors to mark the passing of time, and hopefully our growth and evolution. We can compare how we feel this year with how we felt last year, and look forward and hope and plan for how we would like to feel next year. Anniversaries, birthdays and festivals all break the year up into more of a manageable landscape instead of a vast expanse of time, and they also give us points to pause, reflect, reconsider. They help us to structure our storytelling about ourselves and each other and they give us something to catch hold of if we're feeling lost at sea. We can choose, too, in the here and now, to anchor ourselves to smaller cycles which are more personal – the rhythms of our bodies, our breathing – and to try to find some comfort in the recognition that these cycles are echoed in the natural world around us, in the shifting of day to dusk and dusk to night, or the new growth and eventual death of the leaves on the trees around us.

I find the evidence base of psychology to be a helpful anchor too. I hope this book will introduce you to some new ideas from the subject that you can use for yourself. I've written about some of the studies that unearthed them and I've explained how they've been useful to me or how they can be applied in specific circumstances. I won't be sharing specific stories of the people who have come to see me for therapy, as those are confidential, but I've created some amalgamated stories which will look at issues that cause problems for many people.

If you do find yourself experiencing a greater degree of suffering, one which is getting in the way of your daily life, then I'd like to be clear that this book is no substitute for therapy or other possible sources of help, and I'd recommend talking to your GP or exploring some of the resources in the notes at the end of the book or in the Key Ideas sections at the end of each month. In this book I'm psychology magpie-ing, picking out the shiny bits that are useful day to day. I hope you find them shiny too.

1

JANUARY

Which Way Next?

Decisions, Making Changes and Sticking to Them

January can bring with it a lot of pressure to make changes and decisions. There's often a nagging feeling that something should be different, better, optimized. What are your New Year resolutions, goals or mantras? What habits should you shed or start to cultivate? NEW YEAR! NEW YOU! It can feel exhausting.

The focus on New Year resolutions in January goes way back to Roman times, when people promised the two-headed god Janus that they would behave better. Janus has two faces, looking both forwards and backwards, and is who the month of January is named after. People still tend to make changes at the beginning of a new calendar year and other temporal landmarks like birthdays. Moments like these provide a clear opportunity to reflect on the past to improve the future. They give us a sense of a 'fresh start', which can encourage us to think something new is possible, even if it can be difficult to stick to. Picking a 'one-shot' goal like booking your first driving lesson is a good way to capitalize on these land-mark timepoints, rather than longer-term goals that need continual motivation. Goals which are 'SMART' are even better (specific, measurable, achievable, relevant and time-limited). Despite one-shot goals being more achievable, common New Year resolutions tend to be longer-term and harder – like weight loss, or kicking smoking or alcohol, with 'dry January' becoming increasingly popular. The risk with this is that we pick something so big that we set ourselves up to fail and then feel disheartened. If we want to move towards a bigger goal then breaking it down into smaller steps is a helpful way to go about it, so we can celebrate achievable wins and feel more motivated. January is a good month to be aware of what psychology has to teach us about how we can make changes and stick to them, and also about decision-making and change processes in general.

Although New Year seems to celebrate change and possibility, the reality of choosing to change, and the decision-making processes which go before it, can be really painful. I recall very well a January which felt full of change for me. It was preceded by a long period of having to decide whether to take a job opportunity or not. It was a promotion – it felt very shiny and rare. It also meant leaving London where I'd lived for thirteen years, leaving all my friends, my colleagues, a brilliant supervisor and a job I really loved. The decision was prolonged, in my own head at least, by the organization in Bristol that the new role was with taking ages to send me the confirmed job offer, which put me off finally handing in my notice.

In that time, I would regularly wake in the night feeling a deep sense of fear in the darkness. I'd try logically to solve what I should do: I'd turn the light on and write things down. One night I wrote: 'I keep lying awake or waking up with a jolt, running over all the possible scenarios. Nothing leads to any relief. There's no way of knowing what will happen, no way of hedging all the bets.'

It sounds a bit dramatic, doesn't it? But that's what I'm like in the middle of the night. It's also reflective of how lost any of us can feel in the process of change.

Another sleepless night, I got up to write out an Excel spreadsheet of all the pros and cons of leaving and not leaving. I was following a method of problem-solving that is based on the idea of being able to get things down on paper and see in black and white what the relative merits are of different options.

To do it, you write your different options out, and list the pros and cons for each scenario. You also add how important each pro and con is to you, using a number – you can pick between 0 and 10, for example. So, if having a better job title is really important you can put 8, or if staying near friends and family is the most important you can put 10. The weighting, like this, of the different pros and cons is useful, because sometimes you might have five things that make something seem like a good idea, and only one thing that makes it seem like a bad idea, but that one thing is more important to you than all the rest put together. For instance, if I had five minor reasons for moving, which I only rated 1 in importance, but one reason for staying, which I rated a 10, then that would give me pause for thought.

So I did that, in the early hours of one morning, entering all the numbers for how important things were to me, adding them up. And I found that... the pros and cons were pretty equal, with no massive differences in how big the numbers were. I gave up and made myself a cup of tea and went back to bed with the shipping forecast to try to get to sleep.

I'd tried to rationally problem-solve but it had brought me back to square one. I was left again in limbo, not knowing what the best option was. I tried other things too, like flipping a coin to see what my gut instinct was when it landed on either option – but I knew I was doing it so it was hard to trick myself. I tried talking the dilemma through with friends, family and colleagues, but I still returned to worrying even after I thought I'd made a decision. Even when I used the most logical, rational, decision-making processes I knew, I got stuck. Why?

One problem was it was impossible to imagine how things would be if I left: I could imagine things going well and working out and also things going badly. But I didn't know where I'd be living, who I'd be with, what I'd feel like. The move was an unknown quantity, involving an uncertain outcome, as change often does.

As humans, we don't do brilliantly with uncertainty. It makes us anxious. It can also get in the way of our ability to problem-solve and make decisions. Professor Mark Freeston and his colleagues at Newcastle University have looked at this in the context of people experiencing generalized anxiety disorder, or GAD.

GAD is unfocused worry and anxiety not centred on anything in particular, although it can be exacerbated by specific events.[1] It's a kind of free-floating worry, and sometimes involves worrying about worry itself, which is incredibly tiring.

Mark Freeston found that people with a diagnosis of GAD had good knowledge of problem-solving, they just couldn't use it to solve problems.[2] What got in the way? Being able to tolerate the uncertainty of what was going to happen was a major block. This uncertainty was threatening in and of itself.[3]

This is pretty much what I felt like when I was trying to decide about that job. It led to 'analysis paralysis' where I would go over the information I had, but could never move forward because there was much that I didn't, and couldn't, know about the future. Part of sidestepping these responses to decisions that relate to uncertain future outcomes involves noticing that uncertainty is difficult, accepting that it's not possible to know what will happen, and trying to focus on the present moment instead of an imagined future which may or may not occur. This can take practice, but noticing that we're worrying about something which is by its nature uncertain can be the first step in realizing it's not a productive thing to worry over. It's not something we can think our way out of. Saying to ourselves 'I can't know this' is one way to try to get out of the worry loops we can get tangled up in (and we'll come back to this in July's chapter on existential worries).

Noticing uncertainty can be helpful for small as well as big decisions, if it helps us to detach a bit from the outcome and think about the process or motivation behind what we're doing. With New Year resolutions, for example, we often don't know what the outcome will be, and it can be more helpful to think about what we want to achieve on a day-to-day level, or in the sense of a key aim we're moving closer towards with our resolution, or a key value we want to live our life by (more on this in a bit).

Another reason for us getting stuck on decisions can be the complexity of the decisions we make. The experimental models which psychologists use tend to be tested on very simple decisions, but real life is usually much more complicated.

The decision, for example, to take £5 now or £10 later, a common lab experiment, is quite different from deciding whether to move house. Stakes are bigger in the house move, and there are many more factors involved. Decisions in real life happen in an emotional and social context as well, whereas experiments about decision-making often happen alone in a room of a psychology department.

As human beings, we are hugely influenced by what others think of us and are doing. If our social environment changes, so too can our feelings about decisions we've made. The social context in which we make our decisions creates an emotional background which is often at least as important as the logical things we weigh up. For example, often one of the hardest things about moving is leaving people behind, especially when there's no emotional connection to those friends or loved ones we haven't met yet.

A further complexity is that often the decisions we make don't only affect us. Jean-Paul Sartre, writing in the 1940s, tapped into this when he said that 'when we choose, we choose for others too'. Decision-making often affects a network of other people with whom we are interconnected: both those close to us and others who we haven't met but who may be affected by the outcome of what we decide. My decision to leave my work and home would affect people at work and friends around me, as well as the people in the place I was moving to.

Sometimes the decisions we make are actually *for* other people. Medical professionals often need to do this for their patients, as do financial advisors for their clients. Studies looking at whether our decisions are different if we're choosing for someone other than ourselves suggest that we tend to make slightly more risky choices when we are deciding for others: we see the potential positives of a risk more than the problems with the potential negative consequence.[4] This suggests we can be overcautious when it comes to our own choices.

However, even this isn't simple. Studies show the extent to which we are cautious about a decision's outcome depends on what the context is and who the person is we are choosing for.[5] If it's a medical decision where the potential outcome is dangerous, for example, we might be *more* cautious when deciding for someone else. If it's a decision where the loss doesn't seem so risky but there's a chance of winning big then we might be more gung-ho. So, we're extra-careful if someone else is at risk, but a bit more positive if they have a chance of something good happening. An interesting thing to try, then, when we feel stuck with a decision, is to think about what we would advise a friend in a similar situation.

It's also worth remembering that decisions can be tiring. Decision fatigue is a real thing. We make decisions all the time, often without even realizing it. From small things like what to have for breakfast, to more knotty issues like how to handle a complex situation at home or at work... and then the bigger things: whether to move house, make a career change or some other big life shift.

Whether the decision is big or small, our minds will often work overtime on figuring out what to do and what to say. We can't always see the consequences of the moment-by-moment choices we make, but the things we do, or don't do, have consequences later. Making big decisions can be exhausting, but even small ones can cause decision fatigue.

This is why our willpower is less at the end of the day. If you've made a decision to eat more healthily and then in the evening you suddenly find yourself reaching for the Nutella jar, this is one explanation. You're tired out from making decisions all day and your willpower to make another decision, to avoid the chocolate, is reduced.[6]

This decision-making fatigue has been studied in a whole host of situations. One study found that parole judges tend to be more likely to let prisoners have a reduced sentence earlier in the day, or immediately after they'd had a snack – energy is needed to help our brains make decisions.[7] Another found that deciding in itself is a mental load over and above the research that goes into making a decision.[8] The load can weigh unfairly on some people more than others, depending on what resources are available. For instance, for people on lower incomes, making difficult decisions about what to buy in the supermarket when there are limited funds represents a disproportionately heavy decision-making load which wouldn't be there if more money was available to make the decisions easier.[9] It's not that financial decisions themselves are harder (although they can feel hard), but that the resources we have available to us might make any decision harder or easier. And if we have to make lots of difficult decisions throughout the day because of our circumstances then we will likely feel a sense of decision fatigue at some point. It can help to try to make important decisions earlier on in the day, and to remember to cut yourself some slack if you are feeling exhausted.

A few other strategies can help with sticking to changes once we've made a decision. For example, the more we can do to take the day-to-day decision-making out of sticking to our New Year resolutions, the easier it will be to keep them. Prepping so that you make decisions in advance as much as possible, perhaps by sharing your resolutions publicly to get people to encourage you to stick to Dry January or healthy eating, can help take the load off. Similarly, booking a bunch of exercise classes at once or putting your running gear out the night before might be a useful prompt: anything that makes the behaviour more likely to become an automatic habit. Some people swear by visualization: imagining and mentally rehearsing the behaviour you want to do more of. This can also help you to spot potential barriers and plan how to overcome them.

If we're making decisions all the time, then why aren't we better at it? Why doesn't it feel easier? And what if we accidentally decide to make *unhelpful* changes? Some of our decision-making processes are unconscious. We don't even know that they are ticking along in the background. So we might be factoring in information that we're not consciously aware of.

Daniel Kahneman, from Princeton University in New Jersey, has spent a long time researching decision-making. He has written extensively about the difference between the fast, intuitive system which can be involved, and the slower, more logical, thinking through that we are also capable of.

It's efficient for us to have a quick system that can make decisions fast, and can use unconscious information, including memories and emotions. We don't always need to use conscious awareness. We do lots of things on 'automatic pilot' day to day: brushing our teeth, taking a familiar route, making snap decisions about whether a new person seems trustworthy or not. The trouble is that this system isn't fail-safe, and because some of our decision-making is unconscious it's harder to spot our errors – we can't see our own workings out. It feels like we are making our decisions rationally, but sometimes other processes are at work.

The speedy system is especially handy if we need to make a lightning-quick decision which affects our safety, but is less useful when it brings in unconscious biases that we justify either at the time or retrospectively without even realizing. Biases might be related to outcomes of previous experiences, for example thinking that others are not to be trusted because of earlier experiences we've had. If I'm not even aware of the factors I'm bringing into my decision-making, then I might be feeling that an option is unsafe or unwise, based on other times when I've felt vulnerable or afraid. The situation might be quite different now, but I could still be limited by those previous experiences.

Unconscious biases might also be related to differences between us and other people involved in a decision. For example, biases related to class, ethnicity or sex can creep in and influence what we think is a logical decision about someone else. Although we think this decision is based only on facts, it might actually be affected by beliefs we don't even recognize as belonging to us. We're all prone to cognitive bias, and it is usually unconscious, so we can be both bad at decision-making and fairly unreflective about it. This might be particularly true when we're making snap decisions under pressure, or without consciously paying attention to how we are deciding something, but unconscious bias can creep into more considered decision-making too. The ways unconscious bias can affect our decisions aren't always about other people either. Sometimes the influence is about how we view a potential gain or loss.

The speedy decision-making system which leads to biases and can catch us out is old in evolutionary terms – primates use speedy decision-making and demonstrate bias too, as researchers from Yale University found when they taught capuchin monkeys how to use a type of basic currency.[10] They showed the primates how to use tokens to pay for food rewards, and they also showed them how much food to expect to get for a token. The researchers found that the monkeys were loss averse in their decision-making. They were more affected by situations where they were given less food than had been shown to them, than by situations where they were given more than they expected.

It's actually the same in humans: we are more likely to try to avoid loss than we are to be rewarded by a gain. It takes a greater gain to affect us to the same degree as a smaller loss. I will be sadder about losing £20 than I would be happy about gaining £20. It takes a bigger gain – about £40 – to match the strength of feeling of the loss. This type of disproportionate loss aversion makes us behave in ways which avoid the possibility of being out of pocket, or of messing up.[11] So even though we might tell ourselves a story about why we've made a decision, it's possible that this is a post-hoc justification of other factors, like unconscious loss aversion or bias towards avoiding threat, which have influenced us. I felt quite aware of this with the Bristol–London dilemma. I found myself second-guessing whether I was creating reasons not to go, because it felt safer to stay. On the other hand, if I stayed I'd lose the shiny job opportunity and the chance for a new adventure. I couldn't work out which way my unconscious bias might be fooling me.

I tried something else, after that spreadsheet in the middle of the night. I emailed a colleague, Eric Morris, who had moved to Australia a few years before, and who worked in the area of acceptance and commit-ment therapy, or ACT (pronounced like the word, not spelled out). I didn't know Eric well, but he had given a talk where he had mentioned that ACT had helped him personally in making decisions, and had specifically said that he'd used it when he was deciding to move to the other side of the world.

One key insight from ACT is that our decisions aren't always best framed in terms of reward and loss. It might help instead to think more about making decisions based on ethical frameworks or on deeply held values which are important to us.

ACT is a type of therapeutic approach which has grown out of cognitive behavioural therapy (CBT, a therapy which links thoughts, feelings, behaviours and how our bodies feel). ACT focuses on accepting how things are and how we are, at the same time as committing to living in line with whatever we value most. Individual values differ from person to person, and change over time and in different contexts, but often there are a few key values that are particularly important for how we want to be living our life.

In my state of trying everything I could to feel OK with a decision, I emailed Eric, who replied with some advice. He told me about how he had made his decision to move based on core values that really mattered to him. For him that included wanting to prioritize his family relationships by working in an environment where the lifestyle meant he could spend time with his children.

Working out what your values are is another big question to think about, and of course also involves decisions. It can help to remember that you don't have to stick with these values for the rest of your life. You can come up with your own value words or you can use a values list to help you. Once you've found the top five values, say, you can think about decisions in the light of these. Mine at the time included creativity, adventure-seeking, friends and family, helping others and learning. I reviewed my options with these values in mind.

I found that, for me, some values were expressed more in one scenario but others could be followed no matter where I was. Basically, there was still no right or wrong answer. This is what makes decisions so hard. On the other hand, being able to see that our core values might be expressed in multiple different situations is also something which can help us out of the decision-making quagmire.

Once we accept there is no right or wrong decision, we might also be able to see a decision point as less deterministic. We can decide and then change our mind again if it's not right. This might be tricky, but it's often possible. Doing *something*, however small, can help us stop overthinking – and if it's not right we can do something else. Getting out of the decision-making process loop can be energizing.

How we think about a decision once it has been made can also be important in allowing us to move on from it. Ed Watkins, from the University of Exeter, has spent a lot of time investigating repetitive thinking styles, which involve thinking the same thing over and over (and over) again. This can be helpful or unhelpful depending on the context.[12] For example, returning to think about upsetting things that have happened and how they make us feel has been found to predict depression. That said, we do need to think through difficult things that have happened to some extent in order to process painful memories and upsetting events. In my case, before I made a decision to change jobs and move house, some degree of planning and problem-solving about the future was helpful, but worrying too much about what I had little control over was not. I didn't know what the job would be like, I didn't know who I might meet in Bristol, I couldn't control exactly what was going to happen. In taking the new opportunity, I would be moving away from the safe and familiar people and places I knew. I might hate it. I also might love it.

Two types of repetitive thinking which can happen *after* a decision has been made are rumination and counterfactual thinking. Rumination gets its name from the way that cows digest grass. Just like cows we can chew over and over what we've done or not done. This can be useful if it helps us work out a solution, but it's less helpful if it doesn't and just leaves us stewing.

Counterfactual thinking is imagining what might have happened in an alternative version of the past. 'If I'd done that, then this...' or often, 'If only I'd done that...' We tend towards counterfactual thinking when we're not feeling happy or when something difficult happens. It's not bad in itself – sometimes reflecting like this can help us to make better decisions in the future – but it can also give rise to negative feelings like shame, regret, sadness, guilt and anxiety.

How can we use repetitive thinking styles in a more constructive way? Watkins's work suggests it depends how much control we have over the goal we are repetitively thinking about. If we're thinking about something that is abstract, complex or far off in the future and affected by lots of different factors, then it can be hard for us to solve it using repetitive thinking, and we might be better off thinking at a more concrete level about what to do in the immediate future. So, for example, worrying about what to do with the rest of my life is too big and too vague a subject to be helpfully tackled by overthinking. Instead it might be useful to take a step back and work out what the next course of action might be. The research also suggests that repetitive thinking with negative content – i.e. about sad or stressful things – is less helpful, so it might be useful to consciously try to balance this out with more positive thoughts. I deliberately tried to imagine what would happen if things worked out well, instead of only focusing on my worst-case scenarios, for example. Retrospectively, when I find myself ruminating over things in my life that have already happened I try to notice the thoughts and let them go. Labelling those thoughts as rumination can help with that: 'Oh, there's that rumination happening.'

Just why are we so tempted to ruminate over past decisions? I think it's related to loss again, the loss of other possible outcomes.

Going back to a city you've lived in is a bit like seeing an ex. They somehow always seem to show off to you – let themselves be seen in their fittest, most thoughtful, well-dressed state. Stepping off the train at Paddington, the bustle of the crowds on the platform and the smell of the Underground as I go down the stairs makes me feel alive in a way that is specific to London. I love the bright lights, wide streets, flash window displays and people walking with a purpose, the feeling that things are moving faster than everywhere else, that you are somehow ahead.

I did take the new job and move to Bristol. I moved in January (NEW YEAR! NEW YOU!) when it was tipping it down with rain and I was told off by the driver of a National Express coach for having too much luggage. 'You're not supposed to move house on these,' he said.

For everything we say yes to, we are often saying no to something else. To say yes to a new adventure in Bristol I had to say no to my comfortable life in London. To say yes to my comfortable life in London I had to say no to my new adventure in Bristol. Sometimes it's helpful to acknowledge the loss that comes with any decision.

When I go back now and travel through London it feels like someone is holding up a flick book of memories in front of my face. There is that street where I used to live, the café where they knew me, that bar where I had that awful date, the flat where that amazing party was, the bus route where I cried all the way to Camberwell Green, the street where the flower market is every Saturday, the coach station where I was sick. I still sometimes wonder what would have happened if I'd stayed, and despite feeling happy where I am I still sometimes mourn the losses that go with the move.

But alongside the losses that accompany decisions and change, there is often much to gain. In my case a more peaceful pace of living, less frantic, cosier, somehow less lonely even with fewer people I know; full of many experiences and joys and connections that I would never have known without moving. I ended up leaving the job I moved for after eighteen months, but I did stay in the city, and I'm really content. I still miss things about London, and most of all many people I love who are there. But many other friends have themselves moved now, friendship groups have shifted, and things happened in Bristol which couldn't have happened in London.

And if I had stayed... there would have been other opportunities which I won't ever know about. Making peace with the loss of an unknown future is in some ways as tricky as making peace with more nameable losses, but if you can trust that you are exactly where you're meant to be it often comes true with that belief. And at least in choosing and changing (or choosing to stay the same) you are doing something, rather than swimming in a stuckness, or making the decision to procrastinate.

It can be tempting to think about decisions and change as a one-step process, as a thing we do and then it's done. But in reality, we are choosing to stick to a change at multiple points in time. There are millions of potential deviations from a path we've decided to take. So once we've decided which way we're going, how can we keep on course?

Researchers John Norcross and Dominic Vangarelli followed the efforts of a couple of hundred people in the USA who pledged to change something about their lives at New Year.[13] They followed them up over a two-year period, after these people volunteered in response to a regional TV broadcast. Researchers called the participants up at one week, two weeks, three weeks, a month, three months, six months and two years later. Participants were asked how they were doing with their resolution and also about the coping strategies they were using to make changes. Over three quarters had kept their resolution at the one-week follow-up, but by two years this had reduced to about a fifth. The authors wanted to understand what had helped the one person in five to keep their resolutions. They found that people who were better at it were more likely to gradually reduce unwanted behaviours, and keep reminders around themselves of the resolution they were trying to stick to. Putting a daily reminder up of the thing you're aiming towards, or the longer-term aim or bigger value which is motivating you, can be both helpful and reassuring. It also stops you having to go through the rationale for the change all over again.

Giving oneself rewards for making changes was also associated with sticking to resolutions. In contrast, wishful thinking (wishing the problem would just go away by itself) and self-blame (getting at oneself for a 'slip-up') were associated with the opposite. Being in environments which conflicted with the resolution (such as trying to give up smoking but spending time with other smokers) also, unsurprisingly, made it harder to make a change. Lots of people reported times when they accidentally went back to doing whatever it was they were trying to give up, but 70 per cent reported that this strengthened their resolve, which is encouraging to remember if you fall off the resolution wagon.

In fact, motivational interviewing, a therapeutic technique used in helping people to give up substance abuse, recognizes that 'falling off the wagon' and having continued ambivalence about making a change in our behaviour is entirely normal: something to be worked with, not something to beat ourselves up about. Part of motivational interviewing is making sure that a person really does want to make a change – for themselves, and not for anyone else. Quite often the process begins with writing out all the pros and cons of making the change, both long-term and short-term, and also, importantly, the pros and cons, long-term and short-term, of things staying how they are. Do the pros outweigh the cons? Or do the long-term benefits of making a change outweigh the short-term rewards of the behaviour you want to get rid of? Imagining oneself in six months' time having stuck to your resolution, and in one year, and seeing what would be different, can also be helpful in working out whether it's a change you're really committed to, or one you think you *should* be making. Visualizing the longer-term impact of your resolution can give you a clue about whether it's something that feels like it fits with you and what's important to you.

Take Mikey, for example. He starts the New Year with an urge to shake things up a bit. He's feeling unhealthy and tired after a Christmas season full of late nights and no real exercise. He just wants to feel fit and strong. He has been getting a bad back and feels like he's getting old before his time. He thinks about what is manageable in terms of New Year goals. He doesn't want to set something big and vague for himself, like 'get healthy'. He thinks instead about what the actions are that he can try to commit to that will set him on the healthier path.

Previously he has tried Dry January but it never lasts longer than a week and then he ends up feeling like he might as well just drink loads. Instead he commits to the Couch to 5K plan. It involves three half-hour runs a week – starting with a mixture of walk–run. The first goal he sets himself is to do the first run in the first few days after New Year. If he manages that then he has succeeded. To help himself he puts out his running kit the day before and arranges to go with a friend. He ends up enjoying it more than he thought he would. His larger aim is to get to the end of the programme, but he knows he might miss the odd run along the way, and that's OK. Having a friend who is also doing the programme helps him to stay on track, but the original New Year resolution – to do the first run – was achieved in the first week and gives him a boost of motivation. When he feels like he is too tired to go, he thinks about how he wants to feel in a few months' time. He wants to feel healthy enough to take things in his stride, and not feel so tired and achy. He wants to be able to go for a 5K run without it being too big a deal. The running is just one part of things, but the more he does the more he is also able to make healthier choices elsewhere. He finds himself drinking a bit less so he can go for a run the next morning. He finds himself asking what the healthier option would be for lunch. One change kicks off a virtuous cycle of other changes.

Sometimes the way we frame a change can affect how we engage with it too.[14] Making a goal an 'approach goal' instead of an 'avoidance goal' can be more motivational: if we're aiming to *do* something rather than *not do* something it can feel more positive. So, aim to cut back a cigarette a day rather than aiming not to smoke, or aim to make healthy choices at two meals a day instead of aiming to lose weight. 'Mastery goals' where we aim to get better at a skill or behaviour, instead of goals where we hit a specific target, can be even more intrinsically motivational: so, aim to do a sketch a day instead of aiming to be an amazing artist, or aim to join a pottery class and give it a go. Or, in Mikey's case, aim to do at least two short runs a week, and do not worry about the distance covered.

Making any change is difficult. It's human to try and fail and need to try again. James Prochaska and Carlo DiClemente[15] described this when they wrote about their cycle of motivation, in which they see us as moving from a pre-contemplative phase, where we're not even trying to make a change or aware of any need to, through a contemplative phase where we are considering changes, to a planning phase and then an active phase where we are doing something differently. As part of their cycle they have both an exit, where we carry on doing that thing differently, and a continuation, where we fall off the wagon and go back to our old habits. This isn't going right back to square one, it's just being human and finding it hard to shift what we do. We might need to go round that cycle multiple times before we manage to do it differently, but just because we're doing the same thing doesn't mean we're thinking about it in the same way. In fact, a shift in thinking might be about to precede a shift in what we do.

It might help to take the pressure off and remember that the 1st of January is just another day. This might sound like I'm saying not to bother but actually I see it in reverse: we can change things any day we like. Each day, each hour, each moment can be a fresh beginning.

For me this year I hope to work on many of the same things as last year, and the year before that. That's not failing, it's living a life and thinking about it as you go. I still use values-based action principles to check in when I'm unsure about stuff. What's the most important thing to me in all this? Which values do I want to be living in line with? And am I happy enough at the moment? Because if I am, then why not relax and enjoy the moment a little more instead of wishing myself into a parallel reality.

Making decisions and changing things is a process, not a one-off event. It's often a cycle going round and round as we fall off whatever wagon we're on and struggle back on again. The pressure for New Year to be happy can mean it's harder to feel contented and easier to feel disappointed or lacking. It's just another moment, though, and whatever we feel at the stroke of midnight on the 1st of January we can be sure it will be transient.

DECISIONS, MAKING CHANGES AND STICKING TO THEM

Key Ideas

1. Decisions are hard, and can be tiring, so don't beat yourself up if you're feeling like you're not sure which way to go, especially if it's a big decision about an uncertain future.

2. Try to make important decisions earlier on in the day when you have less decision fatigue.

3. Remind yourself that you can't know the future and that you can change your mind if you need to. All you can do is make the best decision you can at the time.

4. If you're trying to make a decision, consider some of the techniques in this chapter: like doing pros and cons lists, and identifying your key values, but also remember decisions can be complex and some of what helps can be acknowledging the anxiety and loss that comes with any change.

5. Watch out for repetitive thinking – it's easy to get stuck in a loop of worry or regret. To sidestep it try to actively change what you're thinking about – focus on the present moment instead, or distract yourself. You can also notice to yourself: 'Oh I'm doing that repetitive thinking again' – sometimes naming it helps to get unstuck.

6. If you feel really stuck try doing something – it doesn't have to be forever, you can change your mind again.

7. If you're making changes, make sure you really do want to make a change and it's not just something you think you should do. If you're clear on why you're making a change it will help you stick to it.

8. Do what you can to prepare for obstacles and make changes easier for yourself. This could include making decisions in advance where you can, building in reminders, visualizing what you want to do and problem-solving potential barriers, sharing your intentions publicly and creating routines so you don't have to keep making the same decision over and over again.

9. After making a change try to focus on the present moment and where you are now, and tell yourself a positive story about how you got there which reminds you of your reasons for change. If you can trust that you are where you need to be it can often come true with that belief.

10. Don't be hard on yourself for not sticking to a change – it's normal to fall off the resolution wagon and it's fine to go round the cycle of thinking about it again. Decisions and change aren't a one-off, they're a process.

11. If you're feeling really stuck, remember sometimes it's only when looking back that things make sense and we feel less lost. You might be changing more than you think already.

2

FEBRUARY

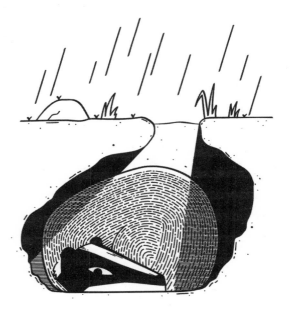

Inching Forwards

Getting Going When We Feel Stuck

The year I moved to Bristol it rained a lot. It rains a lot anyway in Bristol; it's in that pocket of the West Country which is lush and green, thanks to those downpours which strike all-year round. That particular February was bleak, and a lot of it was spent waiting for buses. Where London public transport was fast, efficient and always available, Bristol buses were few and far between and never running to time. The first place I lived was over on the west of the city. I had thought that a 'soft landing' in the posh part would make the move easier, but it meant my commute took ages and I had to drag myself up in the dark, usually rainy, mornings, and take two buses up to the mental health ward for teenagers where I was working. I definitely had days when I didn't feel like getting out of bed. I was tired, and still a bit scared. In the end all the waiting for buses in the dark and rain was a really good motivation for commuting to work by bicycle, when even if it's raining you still feel like at least you're on the move, and alive, and in control of when you're going to arrive.

January and February in the UK are not only wet, they're also dark, and they can seem to stretch on forever. There might be the occasional teaser of a bright blue sky when it feels like the lid's been taken off suddenly, or an early snowdrop sighting bringing hope of spring, but for the most part the days stay cold and the sky is either blank white or filled with low ominous grey clouds. There's no exciting holiday to punctuate the dark days, and it's easy to feel stagnant at this time of year. It can be hard to motivate ourselves to do anything differently (after the initial flurry of New Year resolutions which may or may not have worked out). Happily, there's a lot we can learn from treatments from the clinic room which can help us day to day with this stagnant feeling.

Feeling a bit stuck and blue in a cold and difficult month is not the same as feeling depressed, which is a whole step change of difference. The experience of severe depression is bleak and hopeless. People often describe feeling trapped in a cloud with no sense of how to move forward, or deep in a hole with no ladder out. Depression can suck people's energy and make small things feel unattainable. Even in social situations the other people around might feel out of reach, like you're there but behind glass somehow. At the extreme end, getting out of bed, showering, leaving the house, can all feel impossible to the point where someone's world gets smaller and smaller, as their low mood and self-punishing thoughts get bigger and bigger. If it does feel like depression is around, then speaking to someone else about it is important. In the UK, GPs are the first point of contact for seeking support through the National Health Service, or some services also have a self-referral policy. Speaking to a trusted other in a less formal way can also be a helpful first step to seeking help, and it is worth seeking help because depression can be hard to shake off alone. Even if we don't have depression, some of the ways of managing it can be useful for a less severe type of malaise.

Depression is associated with something called learned helplessness, a phenomenon researched by psychologist Martin Seligman. In his classic studies, a fairly horrible load of circumstances were presented to animals including dogs and rats.[1] Seligman found that animals who were exposed to trauma that they couldn't control learnt to not bother trying to escape subsequent traumas, even if those traumas were controllable. So dogs who were given electric shocks that they couldn't escape then learnt not to bother trying to avoid the shock even when they could. Similarly, rats who had previously been placed in a container of water with no platform to climb out on to, then didn't try to find any way of getting out of the water when placed in a new container, even though that new container had a platform just underneath the surface. In contrast, dogs or rats which had not been exposed to previous uncontrollable trauma tried, and succeeded, in escaping the shocks or the water when there were escape routes available.

Seligman drew a parallel between this and the state of mind we enter when depression is around. We learn a sense of helplessness and hopelessness which makes us not want to bother trying new things. We presume they will go badly, and this creates a barrier to us trying and having the sense that things will go well. I think there is an additional part to this in depression, where if we are feeling really low then the sense of finding something fun is often blunted so that even if we do try to do something that we have previously enjoyed, we might be left feeling numb, or disappointed, or like it's not worth bothering. This in itself can feed into a sense that we are helpless in the face of our low mood.

One approach to tackling depression is something called behavioural activation, which derives from CBT. In this treatment, people are encouraged to increase their level of activity, by identifying things that are important for them, and step by very small step taking actions which help to work towards doing those things. So, work towards doing activities that bring pleasure, or give a sense of achievement, or which express an important value. It's important to keep the steps small and manageable, and it's important that they are things that the person feels connected to.

The first behavioural treatment of depression was created in the 1970s.[2] People were asked to increase the pleasant things they did and the number of positive interactions with their environment. The treatment was based on a theory that people experiencing depression tend to avoid unpleasant thoughts, feelings and situations, and that a vicious cycle gets set up where that avoidance perpetuates negative feeling. It's easy for someone's world to shrink right down when they are trying to keep themselves safe from disappointment and despair. Behavioural treatments got pushed aside for a while, when cognitive treatments came in and focused more on thinking styles, but then, in the 1990s, a psychologist, Neil Jacobson, and colleagues[3] got interested in behaviours again. They set up an experiment to test which made more difference: changes to behaviour or to thinking.

In Neil Jacobson's experiment 150 people with depression were randomly put into one of three groups. The first group were involved in activity scheduling (making changes to what they did by actively planning positive activities). Activity scheduling included people keeping track of what they did in a day, rating these things on how much pleasure and how much of a sense of achievement they got out of them, and trying to increase the amount of things which were pleasurable or gave a sense of mastery. These things didn't have to be big; they could be quite small, like having a cup of tea in the garden, managing to post a letter which had been sitting there for ages, or going for a walk around the block. The second group also did activity scheduling but in addition they were taught to challenge negative automatic thoughts, which are thoughts that pop up unbidden, assuming something negative (e.g. 'That person hates me' or 'I'll be rubbish at this so I shouldn't bother'). The third group did activity scheduling plus a full course of cognitive therapy, which tackles negative automatic thoughts but also goes deeper into other thoughts and beliefs. The researchers found no meaningful differences between the outcomes of the different groups, either right after the therapy or at two years' follow-up. People's scores of depression, as rated by the questionnaires they used, were similar across the different treatment conditions that had been offered. They concluded that the behavioural changes were the most important thing, since the addition of thought challenges and full cognitive therapy didn't improve the outcome.

This is only one study, and I'm not highlighting it to suggest that we shouldn't spend time thinking about anything other than what we do (because cognitive therapy – where we think about how we think – can also be very helpful for some things and has also been shown to be effective in other studies), but more to show how powerful behavioural changes can be. Making changes to our behaviour to influence our mood is one of the basic building blocks of CBT for depression, but I am often surprised at how effective it can be, and I think it can be useful not only when depression is around, but also when we're feeling a bit 'meh' as well.

Let's think about Maya, who has completed her undergraduate degree and is living in a flat share with students from her course, trying to negotiate the transition from student to real life which can come as a shock. Maya's friends are out having fun most evenings, but she feels unable to do the same. She feels anxious in social gatherings, her head filled with thoughts that other people think she is boring and saying stupid things, and she feels low in the mornings, unable to get up and out of the flat even though she knows she would feel better if she did. To Maya, everyone else seems to have things sorted. Even friends who complain about finding work still manage to have bar jobs to tide themselves over, and have interesting romantic relationships to explore. Maya feels too nervous to get a part-time job and too down on herself to go to parties. She feels totally alone despite living with more people than she would have liked, and she feels like she is having a very different experience, and is a very different person, to everyone around her.

That feeling of isolation can be silencing. When we feel like we are the only one struggling it stops us talking about the tricky bits, and we paste on a front that prevents us from properly connecting to other people around us. Being stuck in a vicious cycle of doing little and having less and less energy or confidence is a deeply miserable place to be, and it can engender that same learned helplessness that the rats in the experiment had. There might be a platform lurking just underwater but we've stopped looking for it, so we won't find it even if it's there.

It's no good just telling people to look for the bright side if there's a whole heap of depression lumped on them. Maya feels too low to make it up and out of bed in the mornings. Each morning she watches her alarm clock as the time gets later and later, knowing that if she doesn't get up soon she will have to wait for ages for the shared bathroom. When other people start getting up she stays out of the way so that she doesn't have to speak to anyone, and then when the flat is silent she continues to stay in bed, feeling increasingly grotty about it, but at the same time feeling unable to do anything different. The more she spends her days in bed the harder it is to get to sleep at night, until she is in a vicious cycle of sleeplessness, low mood and anxiety.

Maya is already having a go at herself for staying in bed. Someone telling her to get up is not going to help. But trying to find some way into thinking about what matters to her, what motivates her to do the things she is managing to do and what might help her to try new things, however small, might be a more fruitful way in.

Maya cares passionately about living a thoughtful and creative life. She also cares about relationships: being someone who treats others with honesty and respect. Her high standards for relationships sometimes lead her to feel let down by others, but they also help to show her who she wants to be friends with and how she wants to treat people. In addition, Maya loves being in nature. Her flat has a garden, and one thing she thinks about with her therapist is how to use that to help her to get out of bed in the mornings. Her initial aim is getting up and opening her window so she can stick her head outside and see the garden. This progresses to going downstairs to have a cup of tea in the garden, not every day, but one or two days a week.

Just as vicious cycles can make us spiral downwards in mood, so virtuous cycles can start the process of a lift in mood. Once Maya manages this first step, she feels slightly brighter. She's not running around feeling amazing but there is a slight stirring of pleasure from being outside, hearing the birds and seeing the green grass. It is enough, once she has done this a couple of times in a week, to make her feel like it might be worth bothering to have a shower. In turn having a shower makes her feel much more like herself. The sensation of the water and the smell of the body wash is enough to give her a small amount of pleasure. Starting small and trying to savour activities and appreciate herself for doing them is the first bit of coming out of the slump.

Part of therapy can be about helping people to identify and work towards goals which will help them to feel less bleak. Part of it can also be helping people to spot pleasurable moments.[4] Something I often ask people to do is to use either a notebook or their phone to keep track each day of one thing they enjoy and one thing they feel proud of. It doesn't have to be a huge pleasure or a massive achievement, it could be something small. Things to feel proud of in a day might include getting out of bed in the morning, saying hello to someone on the street, having a conversation you felt nervous about... A sense of pleasure might come from the first cup of tea of the day, listening to a favourite song, a moment where you share a joke with someone. Keeping track in this way serves more than one purpose: it helps us to notice which things make us feel pleasure or a sense of achievement, so that we can try to do them more, and it also helps us to relish these small moments as they occur. We notice what we measure.

I want to caveat this. I think this is slightly different from the 'be grateful' hashtag that sometimes gets circulated. It's true that research suggests making the effort to notice things we feel grateful for is a way of boosting our mood, but I think sometimes that 'be grateful' message can land badly if someone is feeling emotional pain. It can come across as minimizing suffering, and it's hard to do on your own – just turn on the grateful tap – if you are feeling properly low or anxious.

Spotting things you feel some sense of pride or pleasure in is also grounded in research: there are lots of studies[5] that show it's helpful to try to notice and plan to increase activities which give us a sense of mastery or pleasure in our day. I also think it feels slightly more possible than gratitude, if we start small with our expectations.

Working step by step on doing things we know matter to us, or we know make us feel good, even if we don't feel like it at the time, effectively boosts our mood in depression. We can use the same technique when we don't have depression too: doing something which we know gives us a sense of pleasure or a feeling of pride, even if we're feeling like we don't want to, often boosts our mood and our energy. If we're feeling lethargic and fed up, we can think about small steps we can take to get us moving, whether that's making sure we get up and dressed when we're working from home, or finding a way to connect with something or someone we care about: by remembering to spend time on a hobby that matters to us, or by sending a text to a loved one.

If you do find yourself tipping into a lull where you feel listless and unable to get going, it's sometimes a good idea to have a list of things which help you to take small steps in your preferred direction. So start with a list of simple pleasures, and a list of ways of achieving things, which you can just pick one from and use to help that virtuous cycle to get started. It's common to feel like you have to wait until you feel like doing this, but in fact sometimes we don't feel like doing the thing until we've begun to do it. Remembering this can be a real game changer when we feel stuck in bed or on the sofa and unable to get out.

It's not only low mood which can make us feel stuck. Fear and anxiety are also very effective at freezing us in our tracks. It's understandable: when we're scared by something it's only natural to stop and try to work out what is the safest thing to do. The trouble is that sometimes the fears and worries we have keep us locked in ways of behaving which limit us. Having some knowledge about how anxiety is related to avoidance can help us to keep going even when things feel scary. The more we avoid the things we're scared of the less chance we have to disprove our worst fears. Starting small is the key here, again, taking things step by step to try to conquer the thing we're frightened of.

In therapy I might work with someone to draw out a ladder or a mountain of fears, with escalating anxieties placed nearer the top, and smaller worries at the bottom. Whereas in old-school therapeutic approaches people were encouraged to 'flood' themselves by exposing themselves to their greatest fear straight away, it's now much more usual to pick a smaller fear first, and gradually work up the ladder or mountain at a pace you feel comfy with (interestingly, studies have shown that therapists get more stressed with trying to administer flooding techniques than with gradual exposure too).[6] There are now virtual reality programs which can help with graded exposure, like one which helps people with a fear of heights expose themselves to higher and higher floors in a virtual shopping centre, and another which helps army veterans with post-traumatic reactions expose themselves to virtual combat scenarios safely.[7]

For fears like phobias this can be quite straightforward. I had CBT for spider phobia in my early twenties as part of a trial in the building where I was working as a research assistant. It involved starting with looking at pictures of spiders, building up to following a spider around in a washing-up bowl with the end of a pencil, then using my finger, and eventually moving on to holding bigger and bigger spiders. My fear was that they would run all over me, but actually spiders don't really like being on your warm skin, and are more interested in trying to get off you. I wouldn't exactly say I love spiders now – but I am less likely to have to call a friend to come and get one out of the bathroom, which is the situation I was in before (thanks to my friend Anna who once came over just to do this for me).

For more complicated fears it might take some more teasing apart of what exactly the fear is related to, but once we realize we don't have to wait until we feel like doing something a whole world of opportunities can open up.

Maya, for example, has been avoiding going to social events because she feels so anxious about how things will be when she's there. The more she avoids parties or invitations to spend time with friends, the more isolated and anxious she feels. Once she begins to build up socializing, step by small step, starting with a coffee with a friend she feels comfortable with, she realizes that her anxiety about the situation usually comes down within about twenty minutes. She recognizes the feeling of fear but she's able to go to a party anyway, and she notices that the more she goes to gatherings the better she feels about them. She's able to tease apart the different worries that come up for her: that people will think she looks silly when she speaks, that she'll say something stupid, that she will blush and people will think she is foolish, and that she will have nothing interesting to say.

With a skilled therapist, you can design experiments to test out each of those problematic thoughts. You can do this on your own too, but it's often useful to get someone else to sense-check your interpretations of other people's reactions, because anxiety can make us focus a lot on ourselves and notice what other people are doing less (more on this in June's chapter).

Whether it's fear or low mood which is keeping us stuck, our actions, even small ones, can change how we feel. Realizing that what we do can change how we feel is a powerful tool to have in our repertoire, especially when the context around us (rainy, dreary February) isn't encouraging us to do that much either. It means we don't need to wait till we feel like doing something. We can do something in order to feel like we want to do it.

Sometimes feeling stuck can also be about not knowing which direction we want to move in. Not agonizing over two specific options like me with the Bristol saga, but feeling more generally like we're drifting and direction-less. In the bleaker wintry months it can feel difficult to remember what our sense of purpose is about, what we are doing and why. This can feel hugely worrying in itself, as it means sitting with uncertainty (see July's chapter).

Acceptance and commitment therapy, or ACT, which we met in the January chapter, has a lot to say about finding our direction. As we learnt in January, it concentrates on values, the underlying things we want to move towards in our lives. Values are things we hold dear. If we're clear on our values we can get clearer on what direction we want to be moving in, but it's easier said than done.

To try to establish your values it sometimes helps to think about the different areas of your life and what matters in each. If you draw out a circle, and divide it up like a pie with different sections for the different areas which are important, this might help. For example: work, relationships, family, friendships, health, hobbies, creativity... there might be others... then think about whether in each section there are particular things you care about. What is it about work? A sense of connection with your team? A feeling that you have a sense of purpose in your job? Helping others, or creating something beautiful? Maybe it's being able to provide financial stability, maybe it's not to do with the actual content of the job itself.

There might be loads of things you hold dear, but getting clearer on the top ten or fewer can be really useful. In January we thought about how values can guide decisions. They can also help when we're feeling stuck in a rut and like it's hard to move. If creativity is one of my important values then reminding myself of that when I'm feeling lacklustre can help to motivate me to do something, no matter how small it is, towards enacting that value. Similarly, if health is something I hold dear, when I'm feeling like all I want to do is eat cake, remembering my values might help me to mix it up and add some fruit and veggies in. Remembering our values has a different quality to remembering goals, although goal setting can sometimes be useful too. But remembering values is really thinking about how we want to live our lives, not holding ourselves to a particular standard but trying to act with intention.

It's worth, as well, trying hard to keep our eyes on what we are doing rather than comparing ourselves with everyone around us. If we're constantly thinking everyone else is doing better it can stop us trying to do anything at all. Sometimes in life it can feel like others are moving on at a faster pace while we are stuck in the slow lane. Most people feel like this at some point, like they are being lapped by the people they went to school with, or overtaken by everyone they hang out with. A lot of this comes down to the sort of social comparison we tend to fall into all too easily, which social media platforms exacerbate. On Instagram and Facebook most people post photos of themselves having a good time, or looking nice. They discard the images where they are squinting and they don't bother posting about when they are having a boring or a bad day. It makes it easy to assume that everyone is having a great time, all the time, while we're not.

I remember a phase in my thirties, when I was living in London, where I felt like I'd suddenly looked up and around and realized that most of my friends had got married and had children. I felt like I had somehow missed a memo... I was still going out dancing, and the thought of 'settling down' at that point felt claustrophobic to me.

It didn't stop me feeling like maybe I was behind the curve somehow, though, and as wedding invitations gave way to baby announcements I felt a bit out of step.

Not with all my friends, mind you: I had a social circle of people who were also single and out and about, and we had years of fun together. Looking back now, I don't feel so much like I was out of step; I was just doing things at my own pace. There are so many ways to live a life, and so many different ways to do it, but it's weird how often we can feel like we are somehow the only one not doing it right. I really think that the majority of people feel like this in one way or another, and that if we could only let ourselves relax a little and appreciate what we're doing right now then we'd all be a lot happier.

Something to bear in mind is what we are getting from comparisons with others. This might include social media, where it's worth trying to notice how you feel before and after using it. Do you feel better or worse? Do you find yourself feeling energized and motivated or do you find yourself feeling envious and depressed? If it's the latter then ask yourself how you are using it and why. It's draining to compare yourself to others. There will always be someone doing better than you. There will also always be someone doing worse than you, but we don't tend to pick those people to hold ourselves up against.

In real life, face to face, it's more possible to see the nuances of what someone might be experiencing, but even face to face we can miss stuff, particularly if we're already predisposed to find ourselves lacking. When we meet up with people we choose what to share, and so do they. We might be really struggling, but cover it up with an 'everything is fine'. And they do too. But it's easy to compare someone's best version of themselves that they put forward as a public persona, with the worst version of ourselves that we know from the inside of our own head.

This is exactly what research studies have found, that if we compare ourselves to people who we perceive to be doing better than us (having more friends, looking healthier, whatever it is), and especially if those people are getting more likes than us on social media, it can negatively impact our self-esteem.[8]

Likes on social media is just one thing we might use for comparison. It could just as easily be relationships, promotions at work, body shape, pregnancies... How do we sidestep all this comparison and start living our life instead of watching everyone else live theirs? In the case of social media, rather than it being a choice between having social media or not having it at all, it's possible to think instead about how to use it more intentionally, and to connect with others instead of to compare. Are we following accounts that make us feel bad about ourselves or ones that we find stimulating? What happens if we mute accounts that tend to make us feel low? If it's interactions with friends making us feel bad then maybe there is another way of approaching these. Are we looking for the ways that we are lacking? Or can we appreciate some of the things we have that others don't? Can we reach out to others in a different way?

It's not the social media itself or the hanging out with friends that is positive or negative, it's the way we choose to use social media or the way we compare ourselves with people around us. Altering this can be another way of getting going when we're feeling stuck in a rut. If, for example, you find yourself constantly comparing yourself to a colleague in a way that makes you feel bad, can you try to identify what it is you feel envious of and try to take positive steps towards that thing yourself? Or can you shift your focus to your own achievements rather than looking at your shortcomings? It's rare that we tend to praise ourselves for what we have managed to do in a day, and easier to see what is left on our to-do list, but even taking a few minutes to notice the things we have achieved can help us to feel more buoyant.

Making small shifts like this, either in what we are doing, or how we are perceiving what we are doing, can feel too insignificant to have an effect on how we feel or our general direction of travel. Any big shift can be broken down into smaller shifts, though, and making small steps in a favoured direction helps us feel more able to then take bigger strides. Changing our way of approaching how we compare ourselves with others might also make us realize that we're just doing something different and not necessarily something worse. Maybe we're not as stuck as we feel.

GETTING GOING WHEN WE FEEL STUCK

Key Ideas

1. Doing things before we feel like doing them can end up making us feel like doing them. Instead of waiting until you're in the mood to do something that you know you value or enjoy, or which you know will make you feel better after doing it, try taking a small step towards doing that thing before you fancy it. One way of doing this is to give yourself ten minutes to do the thing you think will make you feel better (ten minutes of dancing around to a favourite song, or a ten-minute workout, or ten minutes of writing something you want to write or reading a book you're interested in). Usually this kick-starts a virtuous cycle of feeling better and doing more, whether that's carrying on past the ten minutes or being more likely to do another ten minutes another day.

2. Try to notice and savour those times when you do something that makes you feel happy or proud. Keeping track of these times gives you ideas for what things make you feel good and also helps you to notice the pleasurable and proud moments more.

3. If anxiety is keeping you stuck, try edging towards the thing you are afraid of in a small way. Again this helps to start a virtuous cycle of feeling more confident and being able to do more.

4. If feeling stuck is to do with not knowing which direction you want to move in, try thinking about what really matters to you. What is important to you if you can only pick ten things? Family? Creativity? Love? What is it? What would be an action that would help you to express one of these values in your life?

5. If comparing yourself with others is keeping you stuck, remember that there is always someone doing better and worse than you, and that people often show themselves at their best on social media and when they are asked how they are. You might be comparing your worst day with someone else's best day. And ultimately, even if you are out of sync with people around you, maybe you're just doing things on a different timescale, and that's OK.

6. If the description of depression felt resonant for you, the book *Recovery Letters*, edited by James Withey and Olivia Sagan, has letters from people to their depressed selves, and is worth a read. It's also worth speaking to your GP and asking about options including talking therapies.

3

MARCH

Spring Cleaning

Creating Spaces That Help Us to Feel Better

There's a lot of talk in spring about cleaning, Marie Kondo-ing our living spaces, and generally decluttering. The idea of a beautifully organized space, where everything has its place, and everything has a reason for being there, is calming. It reminds me of settings we go to which aren't really ours: holiday homes or hotels, spas, yoga studios and therapy rooms; places where we can try to escape our day-to-day messy experiences. It contrasts with the reality, in my house at least, of piles of paper, random boxes of stuff and surfaces which are far from uncluttered minimalism.

Perhaps what we are doing, in pruning back our stuff, is trying to clear away the clutter of our everyday lives – our to-do lists, our piles of things to be tidied up, the thoughts that skitter about and don't settle – to make space for a more essential version of ourselves. Space for a calmer sense of who we are: the self who can respond consciously instead of reacting with a knee-jerk to things flying at us from all directions.

It's hard to declutter, though. Anyone who has ever tried to rationalize their stuff, or spring-clean the space they live in, will know how weirdly tiring it can feel and how likely it is that after an hour of emptying drawers you'll be left surrounded by mess, not knowing quite how you got there or how to get out of it. Is it even worth it? What do we *really* know about how the environments we spend our time in can influence our health and wellbeing? Is feng shui based on anything tangible?

Focusing on the way we fold our clothes might be going a step too far, as might putting too much store in the exact position of a certain-coloured rug, but there is good evidence that our surroundings matter, both psychologically and physically. Where we spend our time has an impact on how we feel. Our external environments often reflect our internal headspaces, and shifting what's on the outside can help to change the inside feelings too. When people enter a therapy room they often come with a sense of chaos and a lack of control or safety. Ideally the therapy room and the therapist can help someone to reclaim a sense of feeling contained and held in a calm, safe space. When we feel stuck in a rut and we can't move on, then changing our space can help, shaking things up to have fresh perspectives, a different point of view. We can create a space that helps us to feel better.

For most of us the environments where we spend the bulk of our time are where we live and where we work. My first job, as a newly qualified clinical psychologist, was working at the Bethlem Hospital, which is based in Beckenham in Kent. Bethlem is one of the oldest mental health hospitals, and is where the word 'bedlam' comes from. Bethlem used to be in central London, and has moved location twice, but the site where it is now has a large footprint with a lot of green space, flower beds, an art gallery and a wide-open field. There's a hospital minibus which you can catch from the Maudsley Hospital, in Camberwell, to the Bethlem grounds, always busy both with people accessing treatment and people who work there.

Throughout the bus journey to the Kent hospital site the surrounding streets get less chaotic and crowded, until you reach the wide roads of Beckenham, with more trees and fewer people. Approaching the Bethlem, its tall gates stretch up grandly, and the drive curves past a circular rose bed. The ward where I worked was a five-minute walk away, at the edge of the grounds, past the brightly painted occupational therapy block. The ward was for teenagers, and upstairs was a separate ward for children, so the main entrance for both had been decorated with a big tree made by young people staying there. On the children's ward upstairs there were stencils of woodland animals, and on the ward downstairs there was a games room with a pool table, table football and beanbags. The layout of the wards was fairly standard, adapted from previous incarnations, with long corridors, and a nursing station in each with glass windows all around it, where the nurses could both be seen and see out. The wards were often noisy, and the atmosphere could feel unpredictable. You needed to open doors carefully. But the grounds outside were a good place to go for a walk with young people staying on the ward:

usually peaceful, they gave a sense of space and freedom, an antidote to being cooped up inside.

Much of what we can learn about the effect of the environment on how we feel comes from research in hospital settings. Research into buildings that make us recover better from physical illness goes back to the 1980s, and has gathered momentum in more recent years, being joined by research on mental health settings too.

Roger Ulrich, professor of architecture at Chalmers University of Technology in Sweden, was one of the first to research how hospital buildings can affect patients. In 1984, Ulrich took advantage of a hospital ward with a long corridor to conduct an experiment. In the corridor, half the patients had a view of a brick wall and half had a view of trees. The patients with the view outside got better more rapidly and experienced less pain than those facing the wall, asking for fewer painkillers and reporting fewer minor complications like headaches or sickness.[1] 'Reducing stress, and distracting patients from their internal focus or their obsession on their own pain, reduces the pain,' says Ulrich.

Other studies have shown similar results. In one experiment, bedridden heart-surgery patients were given colour pictures to look at after their operations. Patients looking at an open, well-lit and natural image of trees and water needed fewer painkillers than patients who had no picture or an abstract image.[2] Another study found that healthy volunteers who had a gradually inflated tourniquet applied in a hospital had a higher pain threshold and better pain tolerance when they were watching a video of natural scenery than when they were watching a blank static screen.[3]

If having a natural view is health-promoting in a hospital setting, perhaps this is something that is worth bringing into other aspects of our lives. It's easier for people who live in rural environments to have a view from their home or office that can show them a green space or seascape, but we all have control over what pictures we put on our walls, or what images we have on our computer desktops. Swapping in some natural images is one way to harness some of the scientists' findings on the natural environment's health-promoting properties.

Natural views don't only seem to be pain-relieving, they might also help us to be more creative. I recall reading about the 'green effect' on a trip down to my hometown in Devon. Compared to the city views in London where I was living at the time, Devon felt audaciously green. The hills which were the backdrop to the town were bright and vibrant. Even the sides of a bypass on the industrial estate were lined with vivid green hedges. The 'green effect' refers to the idea that green appears to boost creativity. It sounds like New Age woo, but one study[4] aimed to look at this phenomenon by showing people either a green screen or a white, grey, blue or red screen for two minutes before asking them to complete creative tasks, such as trying to come up with novel uses for different objects, or drawing different figures from the same initial stimulus. A glimpse of green before the task was associated with more creative responses. The study was done with fewer than a hundred people, so it needs to be tested more before we conclude it's a reliable effect, though it may have influenced the colour I chose for my study wall.

It's not just green that has been associated with mood changes. A number of other studies[5] show that other colours can also provoke a positive or negative emotional state. Red in particular has been associated with negative emotional arousal, and blue has been associated with calming us down. This emotional reaction seems also to affect our attention: red has been seen to narrow our attention and blue to broaden it. Some researchers suggest red is threatening for a range of reasons, from more evolutionary-based hypotheses about red signalling danger, to more modern narratives where red in a more academic context is associated with correction. When red, green or black ink were used to write a participant's number on a workbook the red numbers were associated with reduced ability of participants to solve anagrams, suggesting their attention was constricted. Conversely, in studies of creativity, like the one in the 'green effect' experiment above, having a blue computer background instead of red or white was associated with more imaginative responses to a creativity task (asking for ideas about how a brick could be used, other than its primary purpose). Such studies suggest blue broadens the creative range available. It makes sense that if we are feeling under threat our attention is more likely to be focused (on anticipating danger) and that if we are relaxed we are more likely to be able to think about a broader range of things.

Colour is not the only aspect of the natural environment which matters. A study with Danish creative professionals[6] asked them about their creativity and their experience of whether it was stimulated by nature. The words they used to describe how they felt nature impacted on their creative process map on to the aspects of environment which other research has highlighted as being beneficial, for example feeling safe and having a sense of shelter, feeling free, having views over vistas, having a sense of calm, and having a sense of sociability.

The study authors conclude that being in nature seems to help with some steps of the creative process more than others, in particular helping with phases of preparation for a creative task, where we are directing attention to a particular topic, and incubation, where we're unconsciously mulling it over while we're paying attention to other things. This idea of incubating an idea fits well for me. If I'm working on something and stop to have a brief break and a walk somewhere green, I feel it refreshes my thoughts on a project when I come back, even (perhaps especially) if I've not been thinking about it while I'm out and about.

Just why nature should be so helpful to creativity is less well-understood, but there are some studies suggesting that our brain activity changes in response to a natural environment, with nature having a restorative effect. Natural environments and pleasant sensory experiences trigger low-frequency rhythms in our frontal lobes which are associated with lower stress and higher relaxation.[7] Studies that measure our brain's electrical activity and blood flow show this again and again. What's outside does change what's going on inside.

Having a natural view, or at least an image of a natural view, isn't the only way we can bring nature into a building. Using natural materials, like wood, and having plants growing in a space, can also bring nature indoors, as many people noticed when the lockdowns in response to Covid-19 prompted sales of house plants. The Wellcome Trust offices in London do this by having trees growing inside their atrium, and it does make it feel calmer as you walk through the central space. You might have heard of the practice of 'forest bathing', from Japan, which involves spending time in the woods and really paying attention to the sensations you experience there. Wellcome have literally brought a small wood into their building. Bringing aspects of nature inside is one of the recommendations that comes up in a lot of feng shui texts too, and has much more evidence backing it than some of the other ideas.

Scandinavian countries have a history of being good at bringing aspects of nature inside. I travelled to Norway several years ago, to report for the online long-form magazine Mosaic on an award-winning hospital.[8] Coming in to land on the aeroplane, I watched the landscape of Oslo get nearer. It's a fairy tale from above. Clouds give way to dark green forests, which are interrupted by smaller lakes, then larger lakes, then ragged-edged fjords joining the sea. Sandy-coloured roads wind through the trees and rock breaks through in rough-textured patches on the hillsides. The pools scattered everywhere make established forests seem like they are growing up from temporary swampland. There is a sprinkling of houses, gathering mass nearer the airport.

The colours are soothing: the dark blue-greens of trees, the blue-black of the water, the misty blue-greys of the mountains receding into the far distance. White clouds hang still above, with purple, rain-bruised underbellies. There's no visible interruption from modern glass or steel. This is a country where nature is all around you, even in the city, seeping up from the ground, on all sides and above. It is hardly surprising that nature is reflected in Norwegian building design.

Oslo's Akershus Hospital, completed in 2008, won the coveted Better Building Healthcare Award for Best International Design in 2009 and is widely recognized as an excellent example of health-promoting architecture. In contrast to its backdrop of fir trees and hills, the hospital looks imposingly modern, all white with straight lines. As you follow the path round to the main doors, piano music pipes out of embedded speakers. The entrance has two sets of revolving doors, one then another, in an effort to keep heat loss to a minimum. Inside, pale wood is everywhere. To the left are some cosy lamps attached to wooden sofa-shaped benches.

Architect Anne Underhaug, from C. F. Møller, was involved in the team designing the hospital. For her, the wood is not a consequence of the research on its health-promoting value, but more of the experience of living in Scandinavia. 'Have you seen the houses in Norway?' she laughed as she showed me around. 'We build everything out of wood.'

The natural materials are not the only consequence Underhaug attributes to Scandinavian design. As you enter the hospital it feels modern, quiet and very light. If you walk a few metres further in, the ceiling suddenly opens up even more, stretching up several storeys and drawing the eye towards the sky, which is visible through the huge glass roof. Bridge-like open corridors traverse the atrium connecting one side of the hospital to the other.

'Daylight means a lot in Scandinavia because half the year you don't have very much,' explains Underhaug. Regulations are very strict on daylight in Scandinavia, unlike in the US where there are no daylight regulations and it's possible to have an office with no windows. 'Here the operating theatres have windows in as well – everything,' says Underhaug. 'Even the X-ray rooms and CT rooms, MRI rooms, all of them have daylight... People need to look out, they need the daylight. You don't need a book on evidence-based design to know that.'

It's not uncommon in the UK to have meeting rooms without any windows, and offices with very few windows, or with so many desks that not everyone can be near a natural view. In warehouse and factory work, people often work long shifts without seeing outside. In such environments there is no sense of what time it is, just 'work' or 'not work' time.

We know that natural light is important. More natural light has been linked to better sleep, less pain and less stress. In one study, patients in naturally lit rooms took fewer painkillers than those in darker rooms (22 per cent fewer painkillers per hour), leading to a 21 per cent reduction in medication costs.[9] It makes sense that sleep would be improved too, because having a day and night cycle of light helps our bodies to make melatonin, the chemical involved in helping us to fall asleep. In the lockdowns during the Covid-19 pandemic many people reported their sleep being poorer (mine certainly was). This could be due to multiple factors, including stress and worry and less physical activity, but it might also have been related to less exposure to natural light, especially in the winter months, when we were all stuck indoors a lot more than before.

Being aware of the benefits of natural light can encourage us to maximize our exposure to it. When that's hard, for example in the winter months, some people use lamps designed to counteract seasonal affective disorder, or SAD, which is low mood associated with winter. These lamps are especially bright, and can be used for a few hours a day to help boost mood. Similarly, alarm clocks which simulate sunset and sunrise can be a more natural way to wake up or fall asleep. I've got one and it definitely makes the call of the alarm first thing less harsh if a gradual lightening has already woken you up a bit. Soft lighting last thing at night is also important for allowing our bodies to produce enough melatonin to enable sleep (more on this in November's chapter). Poor quantity and quality of sleep can lead to increased stress, impaired immune function and difficulties with temperature regulation. It also feels awful and certainly makes me snappier and more emotionally reactive.

Akershus isn't the only healthcare environment to think about the use of light, instinctively or otherwise. In the south-west of England, in the picturesque Georgian city of Bath, the Royal United Hospital has a very modern intensive care unit for babies.

Laura got to know this unit well, in the summer that she gave birth to twins five weeks early. Her baby girls were looked after in the Dyson Centre for Neonatal Care. Laura arrived there after a Caesarean section, having lost more blood than expected and with a dangerously low temperature. Despite her condition, she remembers being wheeled through the double doors of the Centre for the first time. 'It's kind of a blur,' she says. 'But I do remember the light just really hitting me.'

To reach the Dyson Centre you have to walk, or be wheeled, through the old corridors of the main hospital. It feels hot, that particularly uncomfortable hospital warmth that amplifies the medical smell. Your shoes click on the lino floors and the sound echoes off the plain walls.

As soon as you go through the doors to the Centre, things change. It is light, airy and spacious. Natural wood and soothing greens make it feel more like a spa than part of a hospital. You're greeted by a wooden reception desk, and, to the left, French windows open on to a Zen-like pebbled garden. It smells slightly of chlorine, like a posh swimming pool.

The Dyson Centre has both more natural and more controllable light than the old Neonatal Intensive Care Unit (NICU) that it replaced. A central corridor loops round in a horseshoe shape with smaller rooms coming off it. The ceiling of the corridor is high, with skylights running its whole length, clouds and blue visible throughout. The upper walls are painted moss green. The floor below is a sandstone colour and the walls and the ceiling beams are whitewashed wood, not unlike a sauna.

Finished in 2011 and funded in part by Sir James Dyson, of vacuum-cleaner fame, the Dyson Centre purposefully distanced itself from the traditional hospital look, feel and smell. When they investigated the impact of the newly designed building, clinical researchers had to be creative. Unable, for obvious reasons, to ask the babies themselves how they felt, the team devised new and ingenious ways of measuring the activity of babies, staff and parents. The tricky problem of how to measure the babies' activity was solved by designing special baby accelerometers to fix on to their nappies. Normally used to measure the speed and movement of aircraft and sportspeople, the accelerometers were repurposed to monitor the breathing patterns of the sleeping babies, without any need for invasive tubing and tangled wires. They had to be colour-coded because the initially white-coloured accelerometers got thrown out too easily with the nappies. Once they managed to stop the data being binned, results were impressive.

Ten families using the old unit and ten families using the new Centre took part in the research, along with over forty staff members. Staff movement was tracked with the help of Wi-Fi and infrared receivers. The result? Staff in the new Centre spent nearly twice as much time in clinical rooms with the babies as the staff in the old unit did. Parents visited the new Centre for an average of thirty minutes longer a day. Parents and staff reported feeling less cramped and less stressed than those in the old unit. Some 90 per cent of babies observed in the new Centre were breastfed, compared with 64 per cent of those studied in the old unit. The new environment increased visiting, reduced patient stress and sped up recovery.

Light isn't the only thing that the designers considered, and it isn't the only thing that can help us to get a decent night's sleep. Noise is another big factor in how healthy an environment is for us, both at night and in the daytime. Perhaps unsurprisingly, patients in quieter hospitals report that they sleep better. A quieter environment is also associated with fewer patients returning to hospital after discharge, perhaps because of the additional benefits that sleep brings. Studies also show that quieter hospitals can help those who work there too, buffering against stress, possibly also helping clinicians to sleep better when they go home. Less noise and better-lit environments also seem to reduce clinician error.

The Dyson Centre is eight decibels quieter than the old NICU, and the babies studied in the new Centre slept for 20 per cent longer than those in the old unit. Sleep is crucial for premature babies' brain development, so making baby wards quieter makes total sense.

Noise can really affect us in daily life. Anyone who has had a neighbour who plays music repeatedly, or who shares an office with someone who eats noisily, can vouch for the surprisingly large effect that uncontrollable noise, even when relatively quiet, can have on levels of irritation and stress. Building noise, background chat of colleagues or housemates, and electronic noise from appliances or lighting can also take their toll.

For some people, this toll is extra-great. Some of us are more sensitive to sensory information than others, and the problem of misaphonia is one example of this. Misaphonia is where certain sounds cause people huge distress or a desire to run away, to an extent which others might find disproportionate. Some who suffer from the condition describe finding it unbearable to eat around others, for example, because the noise of chewing is so pronounced. Others might find it intolerable to be in a crowd of people all making a noise, especially in places where sound can bounce around high ceilings and reflective surfaces. Misaphonia isn't fully understood yet, but treatments are being developed all the time to help people cope. If a noise isn't avoidable, then distracting oneself or using white-noise or noise-cancelling headphones to buffer against the intrusion can help to some degree.

We're still finding out why some people are more sensitive to noise and other sensory stimulation than others. One indicator of autism spectrum condition is increased sensory sensitivity across any of the senses, for example finding labels in clothes unbearable, finding loud noises distressing and finding strong smells unpleasant. Sensory processing sensitivity is a separate diagnosis, where the extra-sensory sensitivity isn't linked with the other traits of autism spectrum condition, but experienced more in isolation. Being extra-sensitive in this way has been linked to being more introvert (less likely to enjoy spending time with others), but this might be because sensory stimulation tends to come along with other people: whether it's uncontrollable noise, physical touch or the smells of other people's perfume.

I'm always a bit sceptical of findings that categorize people into introvert or extrovert, when in reality I think we can all show introvert and extrovert traits, with some being more amplified in certain situations. I also think it's useful to think of sensory sensitivity along a spectrum. Perhaps more practically helpful is considering how to manage different levels of sensory sensitivity. If you find background noise very distracting but you share a work-space with someone who loves to have the radio on 24/7, that's going to be stressful. If you find it relaxing to burn incense sticks but you live with someone who finds the smell overpowering, that's going to be annoying. Some ways of making our workplaces and homes comfortable to be in involves thinking about how to compromise with the other people sharing those spaces, and whether to adapt (wearing noise-cancelling headphones or practising mindfulness instead of snapping) or ask (assertively, not aggressively) for our needs to be met. Sometimes there's a compromise. It's hard to write if you are listening to music which has words in it (the tasks interfere with each other), but listening to music without lyrics might be a workable compromise, for example.

The same kind of individual variation is also true of other aspects of the environment. We suit different places. Some people love the hustle, bustle and anonymity of the city and some love the quiet and space of the countryside. The research suggests that natural environments are better for our wellbeing than urban ones, which are noisier, have less clean air and fewer green spaces. But one large study in London showed that the impact of green spaces in an urban environment is larger on people who tend to be more impulsive in their nature. The study asked participants to rate their mood and to answer questions about their immediate environment, and GPS geotagging was used to monitor their exact location through a week-long trial. The results showed significant effects on mental wellbeing, both immediately and throughout the week, from being exposed to natural features such as trees, sky and birdsong. Those natural environmental triggers were shown to have a bigger effect on people who had scored higher on measures of general impulsivity – who were more likely to make quick decisions rather than to think them through. The soothing effect was more pronounced in people who perhaps needed to be soothed more.[10]

It feels intuitively right that low noise, natural light and natural views are good for us, but to understand why we need to know more about the biology of our bodies. There are three main systems in the body that are involved in maintaining health: the nervous system, the hormone (endocrine) system and the immune system. These are in a triangle of communication, each interacting with the others. Anything that affects one system can affect the other two, and anything that changes how we feel emotionally can have an impact on our physical health as well.

A healing environment is one which has a calming effect on the central nervous system. Swapping a stressful environment for soothing natural colours, landscapes and sounds helps to calm the nervous system. Cutting down excitatory and stressful stimuli, like loud noise, bright light and threatening colours, will reduce the likelihood of the stress hormone systems being triggered. By contrast, in an environment with loud, unpredictable noise, harsh lighting and loud colours stress is detected by our nervous system, which communicates with our hormone system to increase stress hormones, such as cortisol, adrenaline and noradrenaline (epinephrine). These hormones activate organs and tissues including our lungs, heart and skeletal muscles, getting us ready to either fight or flee from the immediate threat – be it physical or psychological.

At the same time, these stress hormones suppress systems in the body that aren't immediately necessary for fight or flight. These 'non-essentials' include sex hormones, growth hormones, thyroid hormones and also the immune system. Whenever we are stressed out our immune system is being compromised. While this works well in the short term if we are in danger, conserving energy and allowing us to react, it is not good for us in response to chronic (ongoing, longer-term) stress. It sets off a whole cascade of events which can become harmful.

One of these events is the inflammatory immune response. Studies of adult survivors of childhood trauma, using massive cohorts of people from Dunedin, New Zealand, have compared adults who have been maltreated as children with adults who haven't.[11] The adults with adverse childhood experiences had higher levels of the inflammatory blood biomarkers that indicate immune system activation. This immune response is vital for the body to fight disease in the short term, but its presence longer-term is harmful, and has been associated with chronic, age-related illnesses including cardiovascular disease, type 2 diabetes, some forms of cancer, and dementia.

Chronic stress can happen at any age, not only in response to childhood adversity. People whose everyday jobs keep piling on the pressure are especially vulnerable: those such as combat soldiers, firefighters, air traffic controllers, police officers and A&E staff. But chronically stressful environments can happen anywhere, including in any open-plan office where there is no privacy or sense of thinking space and time.

Hot-desking, an increasingly common office practice, is not always that good for us,[12] which makes sense when we think about how unsettling it can feel to go into work and not know if you will have a space to sit. We're territorial at heart, and having to move office or desk can often feel like more than just being asked to relocate. It can give us a sense that we aren't safe, or valued at work, and stop us from relaxing and feeling that we have a clear place. Studies which look at how people feel about shared office environments have found that although there are benefits from the increased sense of support that comes from sharing a workplace, in the hot-desking scenario these are outweighed by the demands of uncooperative behaviours, distraction, mistrust of colleagues and the possibility of negative relationships.[13] There's a sweet spot where we can offload and feel looked after by colleagues, rather than feeling isolated and alone, but like many things moderation is key, and it can tip over into feeling stressful. Also tricky is when some staff have to hot-desk and some staff don't, which can create a hierarchy of those who have ownership of a space and those who have to pack up all their things at the end of every day.[14] I know I prefer being able to anticipate where I can sit when I go into somewhere I work, although I'm happy sharing a desk. Pure hot-desking reminds me of days as a trainee psychologist feeling a bit like you had to beg for a bit of space to work in, in a busy office. It felt slightly stressful, and probably wasted time too.

Lots of jobs involve making decisions which are stressful. Hospital staff working in acute settings, or people making decisions about large sums of money on the trading floor, all have to be alert enough to make quick decisions based on the information available. It might be tempting to think that we need some level of stress in these environments to help decisions to be fast-paced and responsive, but actually higher levels of stress usually lead to worse decisions. We tend to rely more on automatic thinking styles, which can be biased (as we thought about in January), rather than higher-level cognitive processes. So there's a case for making the stock-market trading floor more relaxing too.

The idea of creating an environment which allows our nervous system to feel soothed, which makes us feel safe, is one which threads through many of the environments we've already thought about. The Bethlem Hospital was one of the original asylums. Although that word has become scary and stigmatizing in some contexts, its real meaning is a place of refuge. The idea of being outside of the city, surrounded by green spaces, is in some ways soothing. The more we can make our mental and physical healthcare buildings places where people feel a sense of relaxation and safety, the better; and the same for the buildings we work and live in.

This is something the Dyson NICU designers thought about too. Looking at the original sketches for the unit, one of them stands out. The architect has drawn the building like a hug, its arms enveloping a baby. The architecture was inspired by literature from attachment theory which explains how as infants we attach to our primary caregivers, using them as a secure base from which to explore the world, and returning to them when we are afraid, ill or in need of care and reassurance. The building was built to be like a great big caregiver, providing a place of safety for infants and families.

In contrast, the design principles in typical healthcare environments, and in many of our workplaces, inadvertently make people more stressed, with bright lights, low ceilings, noisy echoey floors and hardly any privacy. They are the opposite of soothing: they result in hyperarousal.

Anything we can do at work or at home which creates more of a soothing atmosphere can be helpful. Taking in a favourite cushion or blanket to your workspace, creating cosy corners in your home: these are small things that might make a big difference to how you feel day to day. Thinking about sound, how you can minimize sounds which are distracting or annoying, even if they are low background noise, can also help. And trying to make the lighting bright enough to let you see what you need to but without using glaring overhead lights can help too: spot lamps are great for this, as is trying to make the most of whatever natural light is accessible. Getting the balance of having a clear desk or bedside table, but one which also has the odd familiar and treasured object on it, can also feel soothing.

Learning from healthier healthcare environments has been going on for years. In 1901 New York's Tenement House Act made it mandatory for all bedrooms in newly constructed tenement buildings to have direct access to natural light and fresh air. The legislation drew on the design of sanitoriums which were springing up in North America and Europe, many of which prioritized rest, sunshine, fresh air and healthy food as ways of improving conditions such as tuberculosis. These same principles also affected school design: educational buildings around that period tended to consider how pupils could access fresh air and natural light. This continued for many years, until the school buildings of the 1960s and 1970s, when unnatural materials were used more, and key principles of access to light and fresh air were lost. Fluorescent lighting became more of the norm, and fresh air less of a priority.

The early 1980s was also the time when the World Health Organization introduced the definition of 'sick building syndrome', to describe symptoms arising from chemicals used in building design. School design has gone full circle again now, with fresh air, greenery, natural light and low noise levels being highlighted as helpful for student health and learning. Stimulation available in the environment is also important: the best learning environments are moderately stimulating but uncluttered. Research into the impact of building design shows that students studying in environments which support these elements learn and remember better.[15] Designs don't have to be costly, but thinking about how to bring the natural elements in and get the level of stimulation right can be really effective. It makes me think of some of the 'temporary' classrooms I was taught in, in the 1990s, which had been there for twenty years already and likely lasted at least twenty years after I had left. Designers of more thoughtful modular classrooms today have worked hard to get these seen as more permanent structures, because of the impact on learning and wellbeing, and the likelihood of them sticking around for much longer than the word 'temporary' suggests.

There's an interesting balance to be struck in making an environment therapeutic. That balance which the school research has found is needed, between stimulation and clutter, is not the only dilemma. We need a space which allows us to feel soothed, but we also often need a space to have some degree of flexibility – to allow both sociability and privacy. In an office this means not everything should be open-plan; there need to be some nooks that people can tuck themselves away in too. In a home it's similar: some light and airiness is good, but so is having a cosy corner.

In Norway, at Akershus, one side of the hospital houses the wards, the other the treatment buildings. Through the middle runs a large glass-covered atrium, with shops, cafés and a hairdresser. The central 'street' is a principle copied from other Scandinavian hospitals and allows more normal social interaction in a central fluid space. Smaller, more private places come off the main street, including a quiet chapel, and all areas are built with flexibility in mind. The different parts of the hospital are designed so that wards are near other wards with similar functions.

Back at the Dyson Centre in Bath they incorporated social spaces with comfortable, movable furniture which encourages people to speak to other patients, and places with more privacy where family and friends can visit, like single-bed rooms or secluded areas which can be screened off.

At home the range of activities we'll want to be involved in won't be quite as varied, but we still commonly have spaces which we use for different purposes. More sociable areas can benefit from being open-plan, while more private areas need to have a degree of intimacy. At work we benefit from having a mix of sociable spaces, like a shared kettle and tea-making facilities, and quieter spaces where we can work and think, or have small meetings.

We also need a balance between simplicity and complexity, the familiar and the new, to have adequate levels of stimulation from our environment. A bland box of a room can feel a bit depressing. Even rooms that we love, when we've been in them for too long, might start to feel claustrophobic and make us long for something new.

It might be hard to cultivate a sense of mystery in our own home, especially when we're spending a lot of time there, but the principle of having some spaces that are hidden or surprising in some way can still be thought about, even if it's a foldaway desk or a screened-off part of the garden. Similarly in workplaces, any way of adding fun or flexibility in a space can be helpful, from meeting rooms which use unexpected decor to screen off the view of the office, to tucked-away spaces for a quiet cup of coffee and a jot in a notebook. Spaces which reveal themselves gradually can be full of delight. Moving spaces around can also help to bring a feeling of freshness to a familiar environment.

This mix of uses is something that isn't often thought about in workplaces, and perhaps also not at home, but the idea of having spaces that meet different needs can be a really positive one. It's harder in some rooms than others – I'm not suggesting using your bath as a bed – but adding a chair to a bathroom or bedroom if you have room for it, and making a cosy corner where you can sit if you want to, can be a nice alternative space. Anyone who was home-working through the Covid-19 pandemic will probably have needed to create additional workspaces in whatever room they had available, and may have discovered a small foldaway desk can be surprisingly effective.

The opposite of a therapeutic environment is sadly all too common. One which makes us feel claustrophobic and unsafe, with high levels of unpredictable noise, harsh lights and a lack of control over whether we are in an open space or not. Many workplaces are like this, and so, sadly, are many healthcare settings, and some homes.

The first psychology training placement I ever had was treating adults experiencing depression and anxiety. The clinic was based in an old hospital and the service was due to be moved. As trainees, eight of us shared a room with two desks, one filing cabinet and three chairs. Like most services, we needed to book rooms in advance to see people in. It was hard to book the same room each time, so we took pot luck. Some rooms were nicer than others: if it had a little lamp or a piece of art on the wall it was prized. Most did not. Grey carpets, uncomfortable institutional chairs, low laminate-wood tables and the occasional spider plant was the best you got in most of them. Some of the blinds were broken, bunched up at the edges or buckled in the middle. The walls were often dirty. The best-case scenario was drab, the worst was claustrophobic and unhygienic. Not ideal for clients with phobias or obsessive–compulsive disorder, unless you were a fan of 'flooding' (that seldom-used behavioural technique where someone is exposed to their worst fear without any graded steps of exposure which I mentioned in February's chapter). It was hard to feel hopeful about what we could do for people in a place that made me feel sad when I walked through the door.

Why do we continue to use spaces that can be so dark, sad and scary to offer treatment to people who are already inhabiting dark, sad and scary places in their own minds? The answer seems to come down to a combination of cost and a lack of consideration. By contrast, the results when funding is adequate and creative approaches are taken can be fantastic. Hospital Rooms, a charity which partners artists with mental health wards to design murals and installations, is one example of an organization which transforms the spaces people are in. Other changes might be made by local staff with experience of sensory assessments and interventions, creating rooms where all of the senses can be stimulated, using imaginative lighting, different materials to touch, different scents to smell and music and sounds which can be played.

We can use these ideas at home too. We don't have to have a whole sensory room in our house, but thinking to ourselves about the sensations that make us feel good, even if it's just putting some cosy blankets around the place and lighting a joss stick, can be surprisingly effective at changing our mood. Smell in particular is very evocative of memory, and a scent that reminds us of a pleasant or relaxing experience can be really helpful in soothing us.

What of the decluttering, spring-cleaning drive? What's inside a home or workplace also affects the feel of it. Even the best-designed building can be filled with clutter and feel claustrophobic. As I'm writing this my desk is fairly tidy, but just as often it's covered in piles of paper, unwashed cups and tangles of chargers. Yet some research shows that a cluttered desk can affect how well we work, reducing our concentration and encouraging our attention to skip about.[16]

Clutter is a great example of having too much of a good thing. Clutter is often made up of possessions which we find emotionally resonant, or which links to things we want to remember to do; in this way it's related to our sense of who we are and what matters to us. We bring our sense of selves into the physical environment around us. Yet conversely that's also what we can feel a bit overwhelmed by or sick of. Too much clutter makes us feel worse and negatively impacts on our sense of home as an expression of our identity.[17] It's good to have some objects we identify with around us, but if there are too many we are overwhelmed. This also goes some way to explaining why sharing spaces can sometimes be tricky: one person's clutter is another's treasure.

For anyone, having an increased volume of stuff can make decision-making processes around discarding that stuff difficult. When we possess more objects our attention tends to flip from object to object rather than stay still and allow us to decide whether to chuck something out or tidy it away. This same sort of process can happen to a lesser extent when we're tidying our homes, as anyone who has tried to sort through piles of paperwork or sentimental boxes of things can attest to.

Some of the studies on clinical-level hoarding (which at the more extreme end means holding on to a large volume of possessions in the home, to the point where a home is difficult to use for the purpose for which it is intended) suggest that our early experiences can have an effect on our tendency to hang on to things too. If we grew up in a household where things were hung on to then we might be more likely to do the same, and we might also inherit clutter from our families. Conversely, if we come from an impoverished background it can also feel harder to get rid of things: more wasteful. In this sort of situation psychological therapy might work to try to update beliefs about the need to cling on to things, and help to identify whether these beliefs are helping us in the moment, gently and gradually, not just throwing stuff out without someone's consent. Emerging research suggests there might also be differences in information-processing related to hoarding, especially the ability to order objects and make decisions about them. In hoarding, people are often extra-good at seeing other purposes for objects, creative ways of using something that at first glance might appear to be inconsequential. They also often have an enhanced ability to appreciate the aesthetics of an object, and seeing that extra beauty in something might make it harder to part with.

All of us will find some things easier to discard than others. For me it's unread books and sentimental keep-sakes (like a drawing on a Post-it note from my partner, or a menu from a special meal) and cards and letters. Asking ourselves if we need something or want something can be a good place to start. If we don't need it, then why do we want it? And does that object really fulfil the function we hope it does? Does it foster a connection to a past experience that is deeply pleasurable? Or does it make us feel nostalgic or clogged up with old stuff and get in the way of new opportunities? Would we give it away to someone? And if not, why not? This can help us to identify if we are holding on to things that we would consider too rubbish to give to a friend. If so, then why are we keeping those things for ourselves? Channelling William Morris, who believed everything in the house should be either useful or beautiful, or thinking about Marie Kondo's adage of whether the object 'sparks joy' are other ways of deciding whether the object in question is one that we need or want.

Sometimes clutter might be something that feels good in the short term but holds us back longer term. We might be distracted from thinking about bigger problems by the environment we have around us, or we might feel like it's impossible to move forward, something that can be both frustrating and comforting. Conversely, a desire to change the space we live or work in might reflect just wanting a change of scene, or it might reflect wanting to make a bigger shift. If we feel our paperwork is overwhelming us is that a sign that work is taking over in our life? If we crave a restful space do we perhaps also crave more rest time? It's not something I do in the sort of therapy I use, but in dream interpretation, dreams about houses are often said to represent ourselves. In a more conscious way, our houses do express something about our inner state of mind, and can also influence it.

Sometimes the reasons why our homes and workplaces aren't better for us are beyond our control, but sometimes there are some fairly small things we could do to improve how we feel in them, which we just don't prioritize. We might feel we don't have time, or we might feel that it's not worth bothering, but the research suggests it really is worth having a look around and thinking about small tweaks that can help us to feel better, physically and mentally.

CREATING SPACES THAT HELP US TO FEEL BETTER

Key Ideas

1. Tweaking the spaces we inhabit can help to make space for a calmer sense of who we are.

2. Think about several of the senses: sensitivity to noise, light, smell and touch. How can you use elements of these senses in your workplace or home to calm your nervous system down?

3. Make the most of what natural light is available.

4. Think about how you can promote a feeling of safety in your space, whether with cosy nooks tucked out of sight or familiar objects that bring you pleasure and have positive associations.

5. Consider how to improve your view. If you can't move where you sit then what pictures can you put up which remind you of the natural environment?

6. Consider using natural substances like wood, and having plants around.

7. Think about how to make your spaces flexible in use, balancing a need for privacy and sociability.

8. Think about how to make your environment easy to negotiate, but still containing a sense of surprise if possible.

9. It can be helpful to reduce clutter and mess; it can enable us to focus better, although we'll all have different levels of clutter that we feel comfortable with. Considering whether you would give an object away can be interesting – if it isn't good enough to give to someone else then why are you hanging on to it?

10. If you feel like hoarding is a real problem for you or someone you love, the book *Overcoming Hoarding* by Satwant Singh, Margaret Hooper and Colin Jones might be useful.

11. If the description of misophonia resonated, you can find out more at the Sounds Like Misophonia website: https://soundslikemisophonia.com

4

APRIL

Nourishing to Flourish

How to Stop Having a Go at Ourselves

My mum has a cherry tree in her garden which goes for it at this time of year – its pink blossoms seeming to appear out of nowhere. Winter is forgotten, and spring is under way. Flowering tulips, new growth, birds singing in the morning, perhaps even a bumblebee or two buzzing by. In April we realize that things have been changing all along, the seasons have been shifting under the cover of winter and now it's suddenly obvious that things are not the same.

Green things grow because they have the conditions they need for life. Water, good soil, sunlight, nutrients... these things provide the optimum environment for plants to flourish. Without the essential elements they need they dwindle. This sense of things alive around us flourishing and growing can bring us a sense of energy and purpose, but only if we are nourishing ourselves as much as we would a plant we were tending and wanting to thrive. Some of how we nourish ourselves might be the basics:

sleep, eating well, doing exercise. Some of how we nourish ourselves might be in what we choose to make the time for: creative pursuits, simple pleasures, a moment of stillness. And some of how we nourish ourselves might be in how we choose to speak to ourselves.

How we speak to ourselves is important. We do it every day, for most of the day. A large number of our daily thoughts involve talking to ourselves, and those conversations can be more or less helpful. They can help us to move forward or they can end up holding us back. Our inner chat is just as important as the chat we have with other people, and while it might feel like it's on autopilot, it's more in our control than we might think. It's certainly more in our control than what other people say to us.

How do you tend to speak to yourself or about yourself? What's the tone of voice you use? Which words do you use? Would you say this to someone else? Usually we speak more harshly to ourselves and about ourselves than we do to others. We cut ourselves less slack whereas we give others the benefit of the doubt. We're meaner to ourselves than we are to other people, and often this becomes so automatic that we don't even notice. Trying to catch ourselves at this and switch it up a bit can reap rewards. It's very hard to flourish and grow if we're undermining ourselves at every turn.

Different types of therapy have different ways of thinking about the way we speak to ourselves, and there's lots that can be useful from a few different therapy schools. Whichever theory we are drawing on, though, a helpful first step is to become aware of how we're addressing ourselves. Our self-talk might sneak out in things we say out loud about ourselves to others ('Oh, I'm so stupid' or 'I'm so bad at this' are some unkind examples) or things we say out loud *to* ourselves, especially when things aren't going to plan ('Oh, come on, Lucy, don't be so silly' is another less kind one, for instance).

We can't always trace things back to a source of where our negative self-talk comes from, and it might not just be one source either. This doesn't matter – it's not always necessary to know where a thinking pattern comes from in order to shift things – but sometimes it's clear that what we say to ourselves in our heads is something we've learnt elsewhere. This could be from our upbringing, our social environment, or from some previous experience. Sometimes what we've learnt early on can outgrow its usefulness: those thoughts might have protected us at one point, but they can inhibit us in other situations. If we grew up hearing criticism from others, we might have learnt to get in there first.[1] It doesn't mean it's always going to be useful to do this. Although it's tempting to think that criticizing ourselves means we avoid making mistakes or that it makes us perform better, it often makes us feel less certain of ourselves and doesn't necessarily improve our performance. It definitely can make us less likely to enjoy ourselves, though. I'm not suggesting that we all go through life thinking we are amazing all the time and never acknowledging our shortcomings, but I don't think I've ever met anyone whose inner monologue is constantly telling them that they are amazing. We're much more likely to have an overly critical inner voice, and this really doesn't help anyone.

It's not just a case of habit. As children, we develop schemas to make sense of the world and other people around us.[2] We fit new information into these schemas, assimilating it, or if we come across a radically different bit of information we might update our schema and accommodate it to fit the new data. As adults we might come across schema-changing new information less frequently, but we can still update our schemas when we need to, and if we are observant enough to notice when they don't fit the world around us any more. Schemas that we might have about ourselves can include negative ones: that we are useless, or hopeless, or bad at relationships, or some other pessimistic thing. Updating these schemas with alternative information can take time and persistence and often a bit of help from someone else, who can help to see more positive examples of when we were quite good at something, or did try hard, or just had a tricky situation to deal with that anyone would have found difficult.

Whatever the source of the critical inner monologue, we can tackle it using some reliable techniques. CBT suggests that actively seeking to change our thoughts can result in changes in our emotional landscape and physical wellbeing.

Some of what CBT involves is catching thoughts that crop up and trying to evaluate them dispassionately rather than taking them at face value. For example, consider Libby. She has a recurring thought that 'people won't like me if they really get to know me', a belief which hobbles her efforts to get close to others. Taking a moment to pause, and really evaluate the evidence for this, might give rise to a mix of different possibilities. There might be an example of a romantic relationship ending after some time, and Libby might have attributed this to her letting her guard down. However, really looking at evidence for the other side as well, Libby concedes that she has had other relationships in which she has been herself which haven't ended: with her friends, with her sister, and another romance which she chose to end, not them. Thinking about it, the best relationships she has are those in which she is more herself, not less. She might conclude that there was something in her last romantic relationship that made her feel very on edge about being herself, but that this might not entirely be down to her.

Sometimes the stories in our heads really dig into our sense of who we are, and they can become self-fulfilling prophecies. If we see ourselves as a failure, or lazy, or rubbish with relationships, then we're more likely to behave in that way, or to avoid experiences which might prove us wrong. We're also likely to disregard evidence to the contrary, so we have to actively work at looking for evidence for the other point of view.

If our inner voice is beating ourselves up about how we've just handled a situation, we're less likely to seek out more opportunities to handle something similar. This can crop up in all sorts of areas. If, in relationships, like Libby, the way we make sense of a break-up is to blame ourselves and tell ourselves we are rubbish at going out with people, then we'll approach the next relationship in a less sure way, being more likely to subsume our needs to those of others (not a recipe for success). With jobs, too, if we tell ourselves that we left a job because we couldn't do it, we're more likely to suffer from low confidence. If instead we can see it as not a good fit for us, or a learning opportunity, or if we are able to spot the things we did do well, then we're more likely to be able to step into the next job with a sense of buoyancy and competence.

In the movie reel playing in our own heads, we feel like we have a 360-degree panorama of how things actually are, but we really don't. Being able to clock a perspective or way of talking to ourselves which could be potentially unhelpful and untrue is a big first step to sorting it out. Then we can check if the evidence supports it, consider whether alternative points of view might be available, and work hard on strengthening those new thoughts and reminding ourselves that they exist.

When we don't manage to take new information into account quite as well, we can end up jumping to conclusions and drawing some odd answers. Jumping to conclusions is a style of thinking which is sometimes targeted in talking therapies for psychosis.[3] Psychosis is an umbrella term for a loss of contact with reality, and can encompass hearing voices, seeing things that other people can't see and experiencing delusional ideas about the world, including paranoia. Jumping to conclusions is associated with belief in delusional ideas. Now, one person's delusional idea is another's strongly held personal belief. A lot of whether something is considered delusional is context-dependent and the only time a belief is a problem is if it's getting in the way of someone's life. When a strongly held belief *is* interfering with how someone lives their life, though, it can be debilitating to relationships and to opportunities that are available. We all jump to conclusions about things every day, but if those conclusions are wildly different from the way that other people are experiencing the world it can put us at odds with them and make things tricky.

Let's think about Toby. He experiences a sense of paranoia. He feels sure that others are out to get him, and in particular he thinks the TV often has messages in it that are targeted directly at him. Therapy for Toby doesn't involve telling him he's wrong. Has anyone ever told you you're wrong about something you really care about? It's very annoying and not particularly helpful. Therapy for Toby might include thinking about a range of different explanations for his experiences and then evaluating the evidence for and against each one, and seeing if this slightly shifts Toby's certainty about the beliefs he has. Doing this at all would only be needed if Toby was being bothered by the beliefs or finding himself in difficult situations because of them.

As an aside, as a therapist I have often been surprised in working with teenagers who have experience of paranoia and delusions. When I've sat down and really listened to the reasons for people's beliefs, even ones which to me sound very unusual, they often include some very common-sense thought processes or tangible evidence. Toby, for example, might feel a sense of distrust for his mental health team because he thinks they have been talking to him through the TV. Only by digging into the reasons for this belief would we discover together that his community mental health nurse had been on the local news talking about mental health. No wonder it had felt personal and startling.

We don't have to be experiencing paranoia to benefit from the idea of being open to other possible explanations for things, and really trying to look around for evidence that goes against our opinion, as well as that which supports it. Even without psychosis we are all prone to jumping to conclusions about ourselves, the world around us and the other people in it, and about what's going to happen next. This can occur in a particularly unhelpful way if we've had experiences where the world has felt unsafe, where other people have felt hard to trust, or where we've felt like events have unfolded badly and made us feel a sense of shame or self-blame. We may have learnt that we are not worthy of good things, that we need to be ready for something bad to happen, that the world is scary and that people will mess us about. All of these unhelpful thoughts can make us more likely to approach a situation thinking it is going to go wrong, and to behave in ways that make this more likely. To take an oversimplified example, if I think that I am a horrible person and that everyone is likely to be nasty to me I'll probably approach relationships with others in a more defensive way, which might make it harder to connect.

This is totally understandable and very unhelpful at the same time. Checking the reality of the conclusions we are jumping to every so often, by actively trying to question what the evidence is for and against our perceptions of how things are, can help. We have to make sure we really try to find the evidence both for and against what we think, though, a bit like we are in a court of law and representing both sides. A question which can help us to see things from a different perspective is to ask 'What would you say to a good friend?' While we berate ourselves for not doing or being enough, we are much more likely to tell a friend that they are doing a great job or managing well in challenging times. Directing a compassionate attitude towards ourselves can feel harder.

One researcher who has spent most of her career investigating self-compassion is Kristin Neff.[4] She characterizes self-compassion using three main elements. The first is self-kindness instead of self-judgement. We all mess up sometimes. Instead of having a go at ourselves about this, self-compassion would have us being as kind and warm to ourselves as we would be to a loved one. We wouldn't have a go at a friend who had made a mistake or not done something as well as they had hoped. We would probably praise them for having a go and tell them they had done the best they could at the time with the information they had available to them. If we can hold ourselves with the same kindness, we can help to take the added layer of being nasty to ourselves away from the difficult situation of being disappointed in ourselves anyway.

The second element is a sense of common humanity instead of isolation. Self-compassion recognizes that we *all* mess up sometimes, and we *all* suffer sometimes. When we feel pain and sadness it's easy to feel like we are the only one in the world feeling this bad. Common humanity is the recognition that suffering and inadequacy is part of the human condition. That doesn't mean we need to grin and bear it, but it means that we are not alone in feeling bad.

Kristin Neff's third element of self-compassion is mindfulness instead of over-identification. This refers to being able to pay attention to our feelings, negative as well as positive, and allow them to be, without trying either to suppress them or to get caught up in them. When we over-identify with negative feelings we can end up going round in loops with them in ways that increase our suffering. This happens when we ruminate or worry a lot (as we thought about in January's chapter and as we'll come to again in June). If, instead, we can recognize that sad or fearful feelings are there, and hold that recognition kindly and with empathy for ourselves, then we're less likely to torture ourselves with ways of thinking or behaving which can end up being actively unhelpful.

A lot of this is easier, as usual, to think about in theory than to put into practice, but there are some quick things you can do to start using these ways of thinking. Try to catch yourself at it when you're being mean to yourself and change what you are saying to what you would say to a friend. If that is too hard, then start by changing the tone of voice you are using with yourself instead, from shouty or snide to humorous or light-hearted.

It's not only the tone of voice of our inner critic that we can consider. It can be useful to properly flesh out, not just what your inner critic sounds like, but also what they look like. Bear with me here if this sounds odd. Externalizing a critical inner voice by visualizing it as someone separate from ourselves can help to make it feel further removed from us and less powerful.

Think about the voice that reminds you of all your shortcomings. What does it sound like? High- or low-pitched? Whiny or shrill? What would it look like if it were a person? I think of my inner critic as a very grey-looking character – even its skin, and wearing a boring, grey baggy suit. What would yours be like? If we can separate this unhelpful inner voice from ourselves, we can refer to it as different from ourselves. We can even thank it, for trying to keep us safe, but remind it that we don't have need of its advice at the moment.

We'll return to compassion for ourselves again in July's chapter, but for now it's enough to think about whether the way we talk to ourselves is self-compassionate or critical in tone and nature. It doesn't mean it's our fault if we're stuck in a loop or being a bit unkind to ourselves, but it does mean it's possible to notice and change the pattern.

The way we talk to ourselves doesn't only involve cheerleading or having a go. We also tell ourselves stories to make sense of who we are in the world. Stories are one of the great pleasures of being human. From tales around the campfire to narratives baked into songs, plays, films and even computer games, we love a good story. The sense of greater meaning we get from being fully absorbed in a good story can carry us off somewhere else, help us learn about other viewpoints, or teach us valuable lessons. The stories we tell, about our place in the world, our relationship with others, or our sense of who we are, are just as powerful, even if we never voice them aloud. Perhaps especially if we never voice them aloud.

Some of the stories we tell are small scraps, making sense of a behaviour or an experience as it happens. They can change too: I might make sense of one thing one way and then change my mind about how I see it once I learn something new. These are sometimes the moments that stop us in our tracks, when something shifts, like a kaleidoscope changing position, and we see things differently. This sort of step-change moment is sometimes the result of changes to those schemas about the world which we thought about earlier in this chapter: when we update our framework for understanding the world in the light of new information. Stories are powerful.

We are constantly weaving stories, and so it's no surprise that aspects of storytelling can be found in lots of types of psychotherapy. Narrative therapy is perhaps the most straightforward about its importance, placing it front and centre.[5] In narrative therapy stories are seen as the connecting lines between the dots of events. I love this way of thinking about how we make sense of what happens. The exact same events can be made sense of in radically different ways, just as the same dots on a piece of paper could be connected in different patterns, or the same stars in the sky could be joined in different constellations.

If the same things can happen but can be described in different ways by different narratives, then it's up to us what we choose to prioritize in the story, although part of what narrative therapy acknowledges is that it's hard to do this sometimes. It's hard for us to switch our instinctive narrative of what's going on. Sometimes we need help to see that there are other ways of telling it. The events that we tend to notice also tend to fit with the narrative we have – we might not even notice some events if they don't fit with our current story.

Take Kimmi, for example. She is convinced that she's not good enough at the art and design course she is studying. She compares herself unfavourably to her friends; when she does get a good mark she sees it as a fluke, and she remembers the times she has done less well than she wanted to, or that she felt she didn't understand a concept, much more easily than the times when she felt pleased about what she'd created or enjoyed feeling in a state of flow while she worked. The story she tells herself is that she is struggling and doing less well than other people. She's left feeling disappointed. She hasn't even asked herself whether she wants to carry on working or studying in the field of art and design because she feels that any options of continuing with further study or work experience are shut down.

Now imagine Kimmi again. Same person, but this time she has a slightly different story. She places more emphasis on how she feels when she is painting and drawing. She sits down with her radio on and finds she can forget about other things that are going on in her life while she works on whatever the current project is. She sees the times when she gets a less good mark as an opportunity to learn, and thinks sometimes she gets a worse mark just before she gets a better score, because she has experimented and learnt something. She notices that everyone in her cohort seems to be getting a mix of marks depending on the assignment that's been set. She remembers, too, that the thing she didn't do as well on was a piece of work she did in the middle of having flu, and she allows herself to recognize that this might have affected her mark. She thinks about how much she is enjoying the course and how she would like to carry on learning, and this makes her consider the option of further study or work experience of some kind, to try out working in the field.

The same things have happened, but the dots have been joined up in a different way. How often have you had an experience where a story you've told yourself has changed like this? The one I routinely come back to is my driving. If I'm feeling nervous about it I think about my mum holding on to the car door and instinctively doing the foot pedals as a passenger, I think about a time I had a near miss on a tricky junction, and I think about how stressful I find parking. If I am feeling more confident I think of how I passed first time, I think of how I've driven in other countries, I think of how I enjoyed driving on Christmas Day on an open motorway. I'm the same person, but I'm making a different story out of what's available to me.

Some of the stories we get come from the dominant narratives in society. As a woman, as a person of colour, as a person with a disability, what are the stories available? Noticing the lack of stories which fit us helpfully can be annoying, but it also gives us an opportunity to seek out alternative stories that might be more useful: examples of other people who are doing things differently. Sometimes that has to be us.

We have more control over our inner narrative than we think we do. Coaxing yours into even a 1 per cent more nourishing voice than it is now is meaningful. It's worth spending some time with this. The rewards can be big.

HOW TO STOP HAVING A GO AT OURSELVES

Key Ideas

1. How we speak to ourselves is important. We are with ourselves all the time. It's worth trying to change this to offer a kind word rather than having a go.

2. We have more control over our inner monologue than we might think. And certainly more control over what we say to ourselves than we do about what someone else says to us.

3. Sometimes it's useful to identify the influences on our way of speaking to ourselves, but it's not always needed to make a change. Usually if we've got a way of speaking to ourselves which is a bit nasty we have learnt it somewhere and it might even have been useful to keep us safe in a previous type of situation, but we may have outgrown it now.

4. A CBT approach to spotting our thoughts and really holding up the evidence for and against them can be very useful in challenging how we are viewing ourselves and the situations we are in.

5. This can especially help if we find ourselves jumping to conclusions about how rubbish we are being or how nasty the world is.

6. Thinking about how we would speak to a good friend in a similar situation can be a game changer.

7. Using principles of self-compassion can be a very helpful practice: trying to be kind to ourselves instead of getting judgemental about who we are or how we've been; remembering the idea of common humanity – that we all suffer sometimes; and using mindfulness to help us let thoughts come and go instead of getting stuck in a rabbit hole of going round and round and telling ourselves off.

8. Externalizing our inner critic can help us to see them as separate to us – someone to whom we can say, 'Thanks for your help but I don't need this right now.'

9. We all tell stories about who we are and what has happened to us. These influence how we approach what happens next. Pay attention to your stories and think about whether there might be other ways of connecting up the events in your life into different constellations.

10. There are more resources on self-compassion at Kristin Neff's website (https://self-compassion. org), and Mary Welford's book, *Building Your Self-Confidence Using Compassion Focused Therapy*, is also useful.

11. For more on CBT, the book *Mind Over Mood: Change How You Feel By Changing the Way You Think*, by Dennis Greenberger and Christine Padesky, is a comprehensive introduction to many of the key ideas.

5

MAY

The Art of Talking
(and Listening)

Using Therapy Skills to Improve Conversations

May is a beautiful month. In the UK it's often the first month when it starts to properly heat up and feel like the beginning of summer. Flowers bloom, leaves flourish, there is a sense of things being alive.

In Celtic traditions, May is the month of Beltane – Gaelic May Day; this festival is halfway between the spring and summer equinoxes, and is a celebration of the return of summer. Beltane roughly translates as 'bright fire', and burning Beltane bonfires and dancing into the early hours are traditional ways to celebrate this time. A festival of casting off the darkness and welcoming in the light, in older traditions all hearth fires would be extinguished and relit from a shared community fire, connecting people together. The promise of summer brings with it a sense of unfurling, coming out into the light and beginning to interact with each other more. With this increased possibility of connection, what can psychology teach us about the art of talking... and listening?

Trainee therapists are taught a lot about the art of listening, and talking. I trained at University College London, and in the first month they taught us the therapy basics. I was in my mid-twenties, as were most of the cohort. We practised with actors behind a one-way mirror so that a group of our peers and a tutor could watch our sweaty attempts at first-time therapy and give us feedback afterwards. At the start of training, I remember feeling tied up in conversational knots in the pub, as a side effect of weeks spent analysing what we said and how we said it. Talking therapies use many skills, but one of them relates to use of language. Some of these conversational techniques can be useful in non-therapy conversations too.

We all have conversations that can get tricky, whether they are personal ones with friends, family or partners, awkward first-meeting chats at a party or on a date, or work-related dialogue in meetings or negotiations. Being able to understand what someone else needs or wants, and to express what you need or want, is no small skill. In some ways, communication with each other is all we have. All of us are here trying to make ourselves heard and understood, and hopefully trying to hear and understand each other. Connecting, getting alongside, feeling like we are all in this together, it's what it's all about. It's not necessarily smooth sailing, though. It's much easier to listen when your own voice doesn't feel unheard, and much easier to talk when it doesn't matter to you what anyone else thinks.

One of the special things about a therapy session is the undivided attention you get. Your therapist won't be texting or scrolling through their phone while they chat to you. How often in everyday life do we try to have a conversation at the same time as doing too many other things? Being fully present in the moment and really giving someone else your attention is a powerful signal to them that they matter to you. It's a simple but effective (and free) way of showing that you care. It's also much more likely to lead to an interesting conversation.

I remember really worrying about the room set-up early on in training. I would make sure the chairs were positioned just so, at a 'ten to two' angle. The intention was that they weren't directly facing each other so that someone didn't feel I was eyeballing them uncomfortably, yet still felt like I was paying them attention. As a trainee this felt important, and I still think the environments we are in matter, but as time went on and I worked in different places I came to appreciate that therapy can happen in lots of different ways and not always in two chairs set out in a certain formation. In the wards for teenagers where I worked for a long time we would still use therapy rooms, but we'd also go out together and talk as we walked, or test out predictions of what might happen in different situations. Sometimes I'd join the young people at lunchtime or for tea and toast, which wasn't therapy, but probably helped with building up a sense of trust and a sense of who we both were. It didn't matter where we were, but it did matter that I was turning up in a predictable way and properly paying attention to who they were and what they needed. This predictability extends to things like not being late, or cancelling sessions at the last minute, which is also something that in day-to-day life can make a difference to how safe we feel in a relationship. If a friend is always calling off plans at the eleventh hour or turning up half an hour late it makes us feel undervalued, so it's important that we try not to do that too.

In the sort of therapy I do, I write notes in sessions (and often ask the person I am seeing to write or draw things out on pieces of paper as well). This helps me to remember what has been said, and helps me in the moment also to think about some of the most important things that are being told to me. Other schools of therapy wouldn't write notes like this, preferring to direct all their attention towards the person in the moment and write notes afterwards. Either way, we're all still trying to really hear what the person is coming with, both what they are saying and also in some respects what they are not saying.

The sorts of questions that we ask someone can have a big effect on how they answer us. 'Are you all right?' is a closed question; it's answered by a binary yes or no. 'How are you feeling today?' is an open question; it can't be answered with a simple yes or no, and invites more of a response and makes it more likely that we will discover something.[1] 'Tell me about how you are' is perhaps even more of an invitation, as it steps away from the usual conversational pattern that we all get into on automatic pilot:

'How are you?'

'Fine... And you?'

'Fine.'

When someone asks how we are in day-to-day life we often read it as a general polite expression of care, rather than a genuine question about how we are doing. In the context of therapy this changes, but it can still take people an effort to be able to fill in the blanks with how they really feel. Asking open questions which encourage people to explain and describe and elaborate, instead of closed questions which might shut someone down, can be really useful. It can stop us from assuming that we know what someone is going to answer too. If we don't leave space for someone to answer openly then we can't expect to be surprised by their answers.

Think about the last time you asked someone how they are. Did you have a good heart-to-heart? Or was it a perfunctory back and forth of the same old script? We don't necessarily always want a deep and meaningful, but it might be interesting to play with what you say when you meet up with someone and you really do want to hear how they are. Even with the people you live with or work with and see every day, or maybe especially with them.

Asking questions at all, no matter what sort they are, is also important in itself. If no one asks anything it's easy to assume they're just not interested, as anyone who has been on a date with someone who has forgotten to ask questions will tell you. I did my fair share of internet dating before it eventually paid off and things felt good (coincidentally in the May of that year I moved to Bristol, although I didn't know then that five years later in the same month we would embark on the mad rollercoaster of parenting together). Still, I can remember so many dates where it felt like the conversation was just not landing right. I think there's something about dating in particular where the pressure and expectation can add to the stiltedness of conversation, as if you're both interviewing for a job which you're not even sure you want.

Stilted conversations can happen anywhere, though, even with people we have known for years and care deeply about. Sometimes we can get stuck in a conversational groove where we're just not fully connecting with each other. We might be sitting there wishing the other person was asking the right thing, or saying the right thing, but none of us are mind readers and it's hard to know what that 'right thing' is sometimes. In worst-case scenarios what's said can end up exacerbating the sense of distance, with each person feeling that nothing they say is landing right, or wanting to shut down and stop making the effort to communicate. Thinking about how we can have better conversations helps us all, hopefully increasing the likelihood that we will be understood, as well as the likelihood that we will better understand someone else.

Another technique that's used a lot in therapy is called active listening. This involves summarizing back what someone has said, in their own words, to help them feel really heard. So if someone says, 'I feel OK but I've been a bit up and down recently', you might say, 'You've been a bit up and down recently', back to them. They then usually elaborate: 'Yes, a bit up and down. I'm not sure why but I think it's maybe because I've had so much going on.' 'Ah, OK, you think it's because you've had so much going on...', and so on. At first this can make you feel like a bit of a parrot, but it is a surprisingly powerful tool if you're helping someone to hear their own thoughts for the first time. As Carl Rogers and Richard Farson, early proponents of active listening, wrote: 'When people are listened to sensitively, they tend to listen to themselves with more care and to make clear exactly what they are feeling and thinking.'[2] Active listening slows you down in your listening too, makes sure you really have heard what the other person has said and that you haven't wandered off in your own head for a bit.

I'm not suggesting only having a conversation using this sort of summarizing back. On its own it would get annoying, although it would probably take longer than you think to become really irritating. It's another one that might be interesting to play with in conversations, especially if you really want to listen carefully. Saying what someone has said back to them also makes us pay more attention to it, and it allows both people in the conversation to hear what's being said out loud. If you're trying to really understand someone, say in a tricky situation at work or a potentially conflictual situation at home, then this skill can be helpful. It also stops you from firing off your own ideas about solutions too quickly, or jumping into offering your perspective on something before you've made sure you've heard the other person properly.

I want to be clear that I don't follow this way of speaking all the time myself. If all conversations used therapeutic techniques it probably would get a bit wearing for the people around you, and it's also impossible to always be thinking about what you say in this way. I regularly wade into conversations with my partner offering advice when it has not been solicited, or into conversations with family members where I jump down someone's throat because of something I've taken the wrong way. Being a psychologist doesn't make me immune to the pitfalls of being a human, and maybe that's a good thing, but I still think knowing some of these ideas can be helpful in moderation. Even a small sprinkling of some of them might help to tweak things in a positive direction.

Sometimes in therapy sessions I might be trying to rein a conversation in, rather than encourage it to run away down the hallway. Sometimes, especially if people are anxious and finding it hard to leave space in the conversation, or if someone is ruminating over thoughts and repeating the same unhelpful thing over and over, it can feel important to interrupt. This can also be helpful if it feels like someone is on automatic pilot (which can happen to us all), telling the same story again but not really thinking about it. With only about an hour for a therapy session, time feels precious, and I want it to be a useful hour that someone comes away from feeling like it's been worthwhile. If I let them use up all the time with something that isn't moving them towards where they want to be, then I'm not doing my job. Repeating back what someone has said not only helps me to check I've understood it correctly, but also can help to get my voice in, and then move from hearing what someone has said to building on it and offering new ideas.

It can be quite hard to interject, because in normal polite conversations we're taught not to, but in these sorts of situations I'd try to put the brakes on. I might say, 'Can I just stop you there for a moment?', maybe even putting my hand up at the same time to get their attention. I might check out that I'd understood what they'd said so far. I might try then to point out whatever I'd noticed about our conversation so far. It could be something like 'I'm aware of the time and that you said you wanted to talk about your work today, but we're talking about something else... would you like to think about work or would you like us to spend the time on this other thing?' Or I might ask to show them something or draw something out to illustrate what I think is going on.

This idea of commenting on the process in the room can be useful in other conversations too. It can slightly take the heat out of arguments, for example, if you're able to say, 'I think we're getting caught up in blaming each other when actually we're both trying to solve this problem', or something similar. It can really help if you get to a point, with long-term relationships such as with family members, old friends, or partners, where you are both able to notice and name patterns that you fall into. This is in no way easy, but I do think it pays dividends, and helps to move relationships on, or at least to unpick sticky patterns that repeatedly turn into rows. For example, if you're able to say, 'Oh, I think we're doing that thing again where I'm taking what you say as a criticism, can we just pause for a minute and have a breather?' then maybe this leaves room for the other person to say, 'Ah yes, I'm not trying to criticize you here, I'm sorry if it came across like that.' Hopefully.

Sometimes therapy sessions involve thinking about the way that the person coming for therapy is talking with other people. In particular, being assertive in conversations is something that can often crop up. Being assertive, as opposed to aggressive or passive, is useful to learn, and I wish there was room in the school curriculum for this sort of skill. Learning to express ourselves clearly, to calmly repeat what we need others to hear, and to take the risk of not being liked for it, can help us to get our needs met while being fair both to ourselves and the other person. It's useful in all areas of our lives, but it is a skill which needs practice and time to develop. It can come out a bit wrong at first, and feel clunky or cause more conflict, but it's worth persevering with until it becomes easier and more effective.

Assertiveness training goes back a long way, and was particularly popular in the 1970s and 1980s, but is still used today as part of some types of therapy.[3] It's got a strong research background suggesting it's helpful across a range of different clinical diagnoses, and that's understandable when you think about what it is. Assertive behaviour is any action that reflects someone's own best interest but without trampling on the interests of others. It's being able to walk that line between being aggressive or pushy to get what you want as opposed to just lying down and saying, 'Don't worry about me', at the expense of everything you need. Somewhere in the middle of those extremes is a sweet spot where it is possible to say what you would like and not be a pain about it.

Joseph Wolpe and Arnold Lazarus studied assertiveness in the early 1960s, and came up with four main components: the ability to openly communicate about our own desires and needs; to talk about our positive and negative feelings; to say no; and to establish contact and begin, maintain and end conversations.[4] Have a think about each of these things. How easy do you find them? Although they might seem quite day to day, I think they can be sticky for most of us in some way or another.

Assertiveness is not only about what we say but also about how we say it. Our tone of voice and body language go a long way to communicating how we feel. If I am making what I think is an assertive request but in an exasperated tone of voice with my hands on my hips, then it's likely to be experienced by someone else as aggressive. Similarly, if I think I'm being assertive by saying how I feel about something but do it in such a quiet and questioning tone of voice that it sounds like I'm unsure, and if I do it with a very protective body posture – arms wrapped around me and shoulders hunched – then I'm much more likely to be perceived as very passive and unlikely to stand my ground.

Sometimes expressing our own wants and needs can be hard because of other experiences we have had where we have been unheard, or shut down, or we've been made to feel ashamed or guilty about asking for what we want. I think starting small, with little, everyday examples of preferences, can be a good playground for building up to talking about more heartfelt needs or desires. If this difficulty in saying what you want or need resonates for you at all, then an interesting question to ask might be the same one we just thought about in April's chapter on self-talk. What would you say to a good friend who felt that what they wanted or needed was not as important as what other people do? Would you agree with them that what they want is likely to be less important, or would you encourage them to experiment with asking for what they really would like? The risk associated with continually squashing down what we want or need is that if we do it enough we can sometimes end up not even knowing what it is that we would like, because we're so used to ignoring it that we can't tune into it.

Assertiveness training can involve both thinking about the beliefs we might have about being assertive, and practising assertive behaviours. So, for instance, challenging some of the ideas that might be around about not being liked if we stand up for what we really want, and also having opportunities to experiment with new ways of interacting, safely and with feedback from others if possible. Assertiveness training often encourages us to own our feelings and opinions more: to use 'I' statements such as 'I feel worried' or 'I feel unsure', and to clearly state what we want: 'Thank you, but I don't want to come to that party this weekend.' Saying how we feel or what we want using 'I' can help others to understand what we want and need. It doesn't have to be a blunt 'I want this' blurted out; we can use empathic assertion and acknowledge the other person's situation first. 'I know you're really busy at the moment but I feel sad when we have to keep rearranging our meet-up.' Spelling out what the problem is for you can be useful too. 'I know you're really busy with work but when you rearrange at short notice I end up not being able to arrange anything else either.'

If we're trying these things out for the first time we might come up against resistance, especially, initially, from people around us who might be unused to us saying what we really want. This can be tricky: if you've mustered all your courage and energy to say a nice clear no, and then someone comes back and says, 'Oh no, but we'd really love it if you came, please won't you?' then it can be very wearing to have to say no again. In cases like this the broken-record technique can come in handy. This literally means behaving like a broken record, and just repeating, calmly, what you initially said. 'Thank you, that is so kind, but I don't want to come this time.' If you can manage to stick to the same calm response then people will usually get the message. This technique hopefully helps to avoid rows, but it's also useful in helping you to have a good row, where you have said what you want but not tipped into being unnecessarily nasty about it. It's also helpful if you're asking for something in a work situation, or trying to negotiate different boundaries in all sorts of relationships, personal or professional.

What is a good row? We might have different ideas about this depending on the templates we have from other experiences of conflict, and our views on it might change over time. I used to be very conflict averse: I'd do a lot to avoid having an argument, even if it meant squashing down my own needs to some extent. With time, I've come to see that in some senses conflict can be productive. Part of that feeling has probably come from working in wards.

Mental health ward teams for teenagers involve many different professionals. There are nurses, doctors, psychologists, psychotherapists, social workers, occupational therapists, and more. Everyone has their own different type of training in how to help, and different ways of seeing things. In order to provide the best possible care for young people on the wards I worked on, there was a regular ward-round meeting that allowed everyone to discuss how things were going for each young person and what the next steps should be. The young people gave their views too.

People did not always agree on what the best next step was. But ward rounds didn't involve screaming rows. They involved robust discussion sometimes, if someone felt passionately about what needed to happen next, but all within a framework of everyone wanting the best for the young person who was being discussed. They involved joint problem-solving. Without these discussions the different ways of working would not have been shared, and care would have been worse.

Closer to home, conflict is also sometimes necessary. How do people close to us know that something they've done or said has had a negative effect on us? If we're lucky they might notice, or guess, but it's hard to be a mind reader. It's more likely that we might need to say, and this can risk conflict. The alternative, though, of not saying something and suffering in silence, is also a risk: of ignoring your own desires or not bringing your full self to the relationship.

In effective conflict management everyone is active in trying to problem-solve, and everyone takes turns to listen and to speak. This contrasts with less helpful responses to conflict, such as avoiding talking about a problem entirely, or talking about it with a blaming, attacking or critical style, which often makes the problem seem like something that is located in one individual rather than being an external thing that everyone can try to resolve. These less helpful scenarios often result in either a distancing from each other or the eruption of a nasty fight. Sometimes different people will have different styles of conflict management, and this might result in a pattern such as demand–withdraw, where one person is trying to talk about the problem and the other person withdraws. This can often lead to one person feeling frustrated and another feeling attacked. It's hard, again, to find solutions to problems in this way, and it can leave both people in the relationship feeling unsatisfied and like they're somehow stuck in a role that they didn't want to be in.

This sort of pattern can happen anywhere: romantic partnerships, work relationships, and also within a family. Let's think about Meg and her teenage son, Ben. Meg wants to know what's going on with Ben, how he is, what he's been doing. Ben increasingly wants the independence that is usual for a teenager to crave. In response to Meg's escalating questions about what he has been doing, Ben shuts down further and further, offering little but monosyllabic replies, and feeling intruded upon. This prompts Meg to feel less trust in Ben, and more likely to impose stricter rules around going out. At the same time, when things do happen that put Ben in a bad mood – a low mock-exam result, a row with a friend – he is less likely to talk it through with his mum, and shuts down when she tries to offer support. Meg feels like she is constantly nagging at Ben to let her into his life, and Ben is constantly feeling like he has to take himself away to his room or out in order to get some space. The two often end up having a row where Meg is saying the same things repeatedly and Ben is saying nothing but then storms off and slams the door. Ben is going to see a therapist and in one session his mum joins. Talking things through together with the therapist, the two can agree on what the pattern of their relationship is. By seeing it as something they can talk about as separate to themselves, they are also able to come up with some ideas for what might help. Meg offers to ask fewer questions, especially when Ben has just come in the door, and Ben offers to try to let Meg know a little bit more about what is going on for him.

Being able to identify what patterns are going on in a conflict scenario can enable us to try to sidestep the less helpful ways of relating. Many of the skills that work in conflict management are the same communication skills which are useful in non-conflictual conversations: taking it in turns to speak and to properly listen, giving feedback to each other about what you've heard to check you understand, not trying to jump into solving a problem too quickly, before you've really helped the other person feel heard, and owning your own feelings by using 'I' statements ('I feel annoyed', 'I feel sad'). Being able to identify specific and concrete examples of what is bothering you is also much more helpful than a vague 'You always make me feel bad.' Remembering that conflict can be positive, if it's handled sensitively instead of aggressively, can help too. Conflict can result in creative solutions.

Assertiveness doesn't only relate to saying no or having a good row, it can also help us to manage criticism and compliments. Being able to properly hear criticism and respond to it calmly and not defensively is useful, as is being able to accept a compliment without doing ourselves down. It's easy to have a reflex reaction to both these situations, but with a bit of practice it's very possible to change our default response. Even changing a default response to a compliment from a self-deprecating joke to a simple 'thank you' can make a difference to how you feel, and to how you come across.

Another lesson from conversations in therapy is that of leaving space. Have you ever met someone who you feel almost draws your stories out of you, without really trying? People like this are often super-skilled at listening, and at leaving just slightly longer gaps in a conversation. We're not used to having a bit of silence, even an extra beat, and so we tend to fill it in. When I was training I remember finding it excruciating to leave a pause before asking another question. It's so important to leave that bit of space, though – to allow someone time to think, to hear their own words, and to take in what you've said too. A bit of silence after someone has answered a question with 'I don't know' is particularly important. Often we say we don't know as a reflex, and it buys us a bit of time to think. If you leave a pause, more often than not someone will continue with an answer that they didn't even know that they were thinking.

In today's world of multiple social media platforms we are spoilt for choice for different ways to communicate. In person, but also on the phone, on Zoom, with text, using email... we might have conversations that start on one platform and migrate to another. In the end it maybe doesn't matter. There's no rule to say that one form of communication is better. They might be good for different things. What we lose in body language and the micro expressions of face-to-face contact we can maybe make up for in the frankness that can come from a written conversation. Taking eye contact away is possible in person too. Talking when we're walking, or sitting side by side in a car, can embolden us to say more than we might if we were sitting opposite each other, eyes locked. It's possible to sidle up to a conversation more gently on a car journey or a long walk, rather than announce that 'we need to talk' (surely four words which conjure dread in anyone's mind).

Of course sometimes we say things without saying them. Our body language can speak a thousand words, whether it's an evasive lack of eye contact, an angrily tapping foot, or arms wrapped protectively around ourselves. Even here we can be tripped up if we're not careful, though. My interpretation of what you are doing might be totally out of whack, and if I jump in and assume I know how you're feeling it might be annoying. In therapy sessions I've learnt to ask, especially with teenagers, and often to give multiple options so they don't feel too backed into a corner. I might typically comment: 'I can see you're wiggling your leg, and I'm not sure if that means you're bored, or angry, or just a bit restless today. Can you help me out? What's going on for you right now?' In a day-to-day conversation this might feel too confronting, but even asking if everything's OK can be a start at least, if it's obvious from someone's body language that something isn't.

The way we listen to each other affects how much we feel seen and heard in our relationships. An exercise that often gets used in couples therapy encourages people in romantic partnerships to really sit and listen to the other one, before they go on to say what they want to say themselves.[5] All too often in a partnership we can end up either both trying to make ourselves heard at the expense of listening to the other, or both falling into familiar, comfortable, but unproductive patterns, for example if one person raises a conflict and the other one tends to back down. These patterns don't help anyone, because they prevent the productive outcomes that can result from honest conversations. If you're reading this thinking this is familiar then at least take heart from the fact that the first step of changing anything is clocking it. The next step is trying to do things differently, which takes both partners (and sometimes a helpful neutral other person) and a lot of practice.

Telling someone how we really feel can be a risky business. The way we respond to each other when we're sharing something makes a huge difference to how safe the relationship feels. Research from people disclosing important life events, like a traumatic thing that has happened, shows that if the initial reaction to such a disclosure is negative, or disbelieving, then people can end up not talking about the trauma again for years.[6] This silencing can occur all too easily. While not all conversations are necessarily about big subject matters like this, the way we tune in and show that we've heard and that we care, even if it's just that someone has had a bad day, can make a big difference to how that person feels and how likely they are to continue to want to talk to us about it.

The ways we connect and communicate with those around us can be playful and light as well as more serious and heartfelt. Being consistently in touch, even in small ways, is a good foundation. It doesn't always have to be heavy. Just keeping the conversation going, over time, over distance, means you're still there. It might mean you notice as well if someone else's tone changes or if their chat drops off a bit, and then you're able to check in and follow up if you think they might be feeling down. Asking more than once can be a useful way to override that 'I'm fine' script which can get in the way sometimes – that ends up telling us not very much. Asking again is an example of leaving the script behind, as is asking a question that is surprising or particularly specific in the middle of the usual back and forth. Offering our own experience, as a way of normalizing it when people tell us about some-thing they might not feel great about, can be helpful too. Not as a way of hijacking the conversation and making it about us instead, but as a way of showing that we are all human and all connected with similar experiences and emotions. Helping someone else to be able to say what they are feeling benefits us as well as them: it enables us to feel that sense of connection and understanding which usually fosters empathy and closeness, instead of feeling shut out and disconnected. We're going to think about more things which help us to feel connected in the next chapter too, but thinking about our conversations is one thing which can be useful.

The way we communicate with each other matters hugely in the effect we can have on the person we're with, and also on how we end up feeling as we walk away from the interaction. In a world where opinions can often end up being polarized into extremes and social media platforms doesn't always encourage nuanced listening, taking steps to really hear what other people are saying and trying to find some value in other views can feel like a radical act. As May's sunshine coaxes us to gently unfurl from our winter cocoon, we might be left with a pleasant feeling of facing outwards and beginning to reach for each other. I hope the ideas in this chapter provoke some experiments in mixing up the ways you communicate with the people you care about. Some might feel nice, some might be tricky, some might feel uncomfortable initially and need a bit of practice to hone them, but I hope that trying them helps you to feel closer and more fully connected.

USING THERAPY SKILLS TO IMPROVE CONVERSATIONS

Key Ideas

1. Key skills from therapy can be useful in loads of different conversations. To begin with, take the time to properly listen.

2. Use open questions instead of closed ones to get more open-ended responses.

3. Check you've really understood by summarizing back.

4. Don't be afraid to leave a gap in a conversation. Silences don't always have to be filled.

5. Work on your assertiveness skills: how often are you saying what you really mean using calm body language and tone of voice?

6. Don't be afraid to comment on the process of a conversation; it can move things along if you notice a pattern you've got into.

7. Remember that a good row can be a creative opportunity, as long as we're sensitive about how we give our point of view and try to problem-solve together instead of blaming the other person.

8. Use different ways of communicating and make the most out of the different pros that they all have.

Face to face, text, a chat on a walk or while driving along: they all have their benefits.

9. Keep communicating, whichever medium you use. Just keep the conversation going.

6

JUNE

Summer Socializing

Feeling Connected

With June we are properly into summer, and this season often brings with it more opportunities to be social: festivals, parties, holidays, weddings. We let loose a bit more and the later evenings energize us. The extra hours stretch on and we have more time to do things and to meet people. With all the conversational gambits in the world it can still sometimes feel hard to properly connect to people, though, and there can be all sorts of obstacles which get in the way.

One of those obstacles is social anxiety. Particularly in the aftermath of the lockdowns and social withdrawal that we have all been through in the last few years, any kind of socializing might lead us to feel an awkwardness or sense of worry. We can learn a lot, in this situation, from clinical treatments for social anxiety, the debilitating worries that some people have about how they come across to others.

Approximately one in ten people are affected by social anxiety.[1] This problem often starts in adolescence but can carry on into adulthood and massively affect what people feel able to do and to enjoy. Imagine feeling so consumed with worry about what other people are thinking of you that any times you do venture out to a social gathering, or a work meeting, or even go to the shop to buy something, your thoughts are filled with how you think others must be seeing you. They must be thinking you're boring, or stupid, or ugly, or worse. Thoughts like this are stultifying; they squash our personality, preventing us from listening to other people properly, or being spontaneous in what we say. Social anxiety traps us: we are there but not really there, too busy in our own minds running over the many ways we are falling short, which of course means we are out of step in the conversation and not fully ourselves.

It's no coincidence that social anxiety is often heightened in adolescence, a time when our brains are primed to be highly sensitive to social cues from our peer group. Social anxiety in adulthood can remind us of being a teenager: that excruciating feeling of being so sensitive to what people think of us and to where our place is in the order of things. As we get older and establish more what we like, the opinions of others hopefully become less important, but for any of us at any age it's possible to be catapulted back to that sensation of being the uncool one at school, or the friend on the edge of the party who doesn't know who to speak to. I think most people feel like they are the odd one out in a group situation, and that feeling is powerful and uncomfortable.

Treatment of social anxiety is similar to treatment for any anxiety problem, in that it involves doing the opposite of what makes us feel at ease. In this case that means going into more social situations and, crucially, looking up and around to evaluate people's reaction to us, instead of jumping to conclusions about what others are thinking. Most of us worry to some extent about how we come across – but the trick is to try to shift our attention to other people so we can be open to really seeing how they are reacting, and so that we end up getting absorbed in what they are saying rather than stuck in our own head. We don't need to have social anxiety to use these same principles to help us to be our best in social situations, from parties to public speaking, even if we're feeling vulnerable. Public speaking is quite an interesting situation to think about, because it's a very common fear. It might not always involve speaking to a really big crowd – even speaking in a meeting at work or in a larger group of friends might cause you to seize up.

I used to blush really badly. I still blush sometimes now, but it's a lot better than it was. It wasn't just something that happened when I was little, although I do remember blushing at school, but mostly it was bad in my early to mid-twenties. I remember sitting in big meetings when I was newly qualified as a clinical psychologist, and having to speak in a ward round even though I knew I'd go bright red, because I couldn't not say the stuff I wanted to say about the people I was working with. It definitely got better with practice, but even now I sometimes colour up for very little reason.

Blushing happens as an unconscious reaction to that fight or flight response that we get when we are feeling stressed or under threat. It's our sympathetic nervous system in action, telling our blood vessels to dilate and allow blood to pump faster. It might have social benefits, in that it signals to others an understanding of a social misstep or strong feeling. Tell this to a person who blushes badly, though, and they will likely not feel very comforted. Blushing can feel excruciating. The more you realize you are blushing the worse it gets, and if someone comments on the blushing it goes on for even longer.

Similar to other manifestations of social anxiety, blushing tends to provoke loops of thinking where the focus is very much on yourself. You blush, you are aware of the blush, you have some unhelpful thoughts about the blush, like 'everyone can see me blushing, I look like such an idiot, how embarrassing', and this makes the blush worse. These sorts of thoughts often cause us to withdraw socially, to keep quiet so no one looks at us, or to look away so we can't see people staring. This withdrawal means we never get to challenge the thought that everyone is staring, and we also get stuck again in self-focus, just paying attention to ourselves and how much we are cringing. Focusing on ourselves too much, we can get caught up in a negative spiral of how we are sure that other people think we are boring, or rubbish, or stupid... These thoughts tend to lead to us looking for evidence to support them, so we read people's facial expressions more easily as bored or judgemental, when actually they may just be tired or thoughtful.

If instead we can turn our attention outwards, we might be surprised how little attention is being paid to the blush, or at least surprised by the meaning people are making of it. Taking the focus off ourselves and genuinely tuning in with those around us helps to move us on from the anxious loop we can get stuck in. Most people are usually thinking about their own dilemmas, or worrying about themselves, or are distracted by something else, and are very unlikely to be thinking about us. By moving our attention away from ourselves on purpose we might also have our attention drawn away from ourselves and on to some interesting conversation that stops us from thinking about the blush and allows it to subside. Blushing is just one example of how social anxiety can show up. Alternatively, it might be sweatiness, or shakiness, or not being able to think clearly and feeling that our words are coming out all wrong. No matter what the signs are for each one of us, making the effort to switch our attention from an internal focus on ourselves to an external focus on other people can really help, especially if we are able to remember to spot signs that we are safe and not scrutinized, rather than scanning the room for signs of threat.

I definitely experience this sort of worry loop when I'm teaching a room of students or more recently a virtual room of people on-screen. It's so easy to see someone yawn and feel sure you are boring the pants off everyone, but people come to lectures tired and someone's face when they are listening isn't always an expression of wild rapture. Trying to remember that it's not all about me is a valuable thing to attempt to hold on to, as well as remembering to focus on the information I'm trying to convey instead of thinking about what others are thinking. Or, of course, we can ask how others are doing and get more into a two-way conversation, which can also help to take the social anxiety out of the equation.

This shift of attention, from ourselves and our inner monologue to more of a dialogue, is maybe the most important thing underlying all social dilemmas, helping us to feel more connected in the moment.

Social anxiety is not the only thing that can get in the way of our feeling connected to other people. Sometimes we find ourselves trying to relate to new people under the shadow of our previous ways of relating.

Developmental psychology has a lot to say about relationships and how we learn about them.[2] Attachment theory, developed by John Bowlby in the 1950s and further added to by Mary Ainsworth in the 1970s, drawing on a basis of research with both animals and children, outlines the need for children to have a secure base from which they can explore. Reliable, consistently loving parenting provides them with this sense, and sets them up well for future relationships with the world and others in it. There are different types of attachment relationship that children form with their primary caregiver, and these might influence the way we go on to approach relationships with other people. This is not to say that everything is set in stone: we can reflect on who we are and who we want to be throughout our life, and change and grow in response to new thoughts and new experiences, including new ways of being in relationships.

The main types of attachment relationship originally categorized by Mary Ainsworth are the insecure-avoidant, insecure-ambivalent, and the secure. In a specific sequence of events, called the Strange Situation, Ainsworth observed how infants responded when their caregiver left the room and returned, and when a stranger entered the room and left.

Infants who were securely attached got upset when their caregiver left and were comforted when they returned. Insecure-avoidant infants seemed not to notice their caregiver leaving, but heart-rate monitors revealed that the babies were actually stressed, just not showing it. Insecure-ambivalent children seemed clingy before the caregiver left and then found it hard to settle afterwards.

Although secure attachment obviously sounds much better than the others, most people are not securely attached and this doesn't mean anything bad. The only category of attachment which is more worrying is one that was added later by a researcher called Mary Main. This fourth category is called disorganized attachment. Mary Main drew attention to the difficulty which children experience when they have a caregiver who is looking after them but also hurting them. In the same Strange Situation experimental set-up described above, disorganized attachment is shown by much less predictable responses to a caregiver arriving or leaving. Sometimes these infants freeze and seem unsure which way to go, whether to approach or retreat from their caregiver. For children who have experienced abuse or neglect they have an impossible push–pull situation, where they are trying to seek safety with the person who is also the source of danger. This can profoundly affect relationships later on, making it harder, understandably, to trust that getting close to someone else will be safe. Important to say as well, though, that this isn't hard and fast: evidence shows that even one secure relationship with a caring adult can make all the difference in allowing children to develop into young adults who are able to negotiate relationships and the world around them.[3]

It's not only our main caregivers who we have relationships with; our wider family circles are also important in giving us templates for how to relate to others. We learn from watching what others do, and in our homes of origin we often observe dramas play out with their crisis and resolution points, and everything in between. When we come across others in our adult lives who seem to fit into a role we recognize, it can feel familiar and comfortable to fall into a familiar pattern of relating to that person, even if we don't want to.

Let's consider Carrie. Carrie is feeling low and trying her best to manage it, but there is a lot going on with her wider networks that is impacting on how she feels and how she is able to deal with it. Her relationship with her dad is difficult: he needs a lot from her and they are close, but he can be cruel on occasion. She is never quite sure which version of him she is going to get, and when the mean version is there it's hard for her to put up boundaries to keep herself feeling OK.

Carrie experiences some similar struggles in her romantic partnership and with one of her close friends, where she finds it impossible to prioritize her own needs above theirs. This works fine when they are being thoughtful about her, but makes her feel wrung out when they ask a lot of her, at times when she has little left to give. Carrie holds herself to extremely high standards as well, and berates herself for being a selfish person when she doesn't meet the needs of everyone around her.

It is incredibly hard to start doing things differently when you have a long pattern of behaving in a certain way with other people. For all that it can feel horrible to be in a position where you feel put upon and unheard, taking the step to work out what you need and tell someone else about it can feel exhausting and scary. It can really make a difference to have someone else helping you with this – that you feel is in your corner and able to sense-check relationship tangles with you. Sometimes what we are left feeling after an interaction with someone doesn't reflect the entirety of what has happened. If we're used to always giving way to someone else then not doing this can make us feel disproportionately nasty, and checking out what we've said or done with a trusted other can help us to work out if our feelings are reasonable and proportionate or if they may be amplified, and to check if our response seems helpful or if we really have overstepped the mark a bit. Whether this person is a close friend or a therapist, or whether it's possible to get a bit of a sense of an objective observer by writing down what's happening, some way of getting a degree of extra perspective can be helpful.

It takes time and courage to shift the way we behave, but Carrie took steps to experiment with new ways of being, little by little, and it gradually got easier. Saying no, nicely but firmly, to prioritizing others over herself at all times meant she gradually had a taste of knowing what she wanted and getting it (using some of the assertiveness skills we described in May's chapter on talking and listening). She had to do a lot of thinking about her own self-worth as part of this, and learning how to be more compassionate to herself, and sometimes she felt like she was back at square one, but actually she was consistently making progress towards a different way of being in relationships.

I think these sorts of familiar patterns repeating in romantic relationships are why people joke about going for a man like your dad or a woman like your mum. Freudian theory aside, it's not surprising, is it, that we would recognize and find comfort in people who remind us in some way of our first caregivers? I don't think it's always a man like your dad, though – sometimes it's going for a man like your mum, or a woman like your dad; the patterns can lie in unexpected places. It's also never as simple as this, but it is interesting to think about whether there are relationship roles that you fall into easily which remind you of roles you take up in your family too. The way we first make sense of the world is through the relationships we see around us, and although we can expand our understanding of relationships as we grow and change, those first ones can be pretty important.

Friendships can feel just as intense as romantic relationships, and sometimes the same sorts of familiar patterns can get enacted with friends as with lovers. Friendships are so important to our sense of who we are and our feeling of being connected to the world around us. They are often, if we are lucky, some of the most long-lasting relationships of our lives, outliving the more volatile romances.

Of course the relationship we have with a therapist is also an important one, and it can be a useful place to practise doing things differently. In psychological therapy sessions, it's almost inevitable that I will misunderstand or get something wrong at some point. I will jump to a conclusion, or misread someone's body language, or move too fast or too slowly through something. If I'm lucky, the client I am seeing will trust me enough to tell me that I've messed up. It's a big ask, though, because therapy feels risky and it's tempting to think that the therapist might somehow know best. In my experience the sessions I've had with teenagers are often excellent for this. Adolescents tend to be much more honest than adults are about what's working or not. They often have no qualms about saying that the session is boring, or pointless, or that I'm not getting it. And thank goodness, because the only way I'll know is if they tell me, and it saves us both a lot of time if they do it sooner rather than later. An adult might also take the leap to tell me that they aren't sure about something, but they might also very well just say they want to stop coming and not say why. To be fair, I understand this; there are situations in my life outside the therapy room where I've not been completely honest about what I feel about something – not lying, but leaving something out. I'll never know if taking the risk of saying more would have made it possible to have a different experience in those cases – that's what we forgo by not saying what's really going on for us.

This idea that we all get things wrong in conversations and relationships cuts across several schools of therapy.

The concept of rupture and repair in therapy relationships gives space to the importance of being able to mess up, and then work to overcome that mess. Being able to do this in therapy means you're able to practise this for the real world too, and it's so incredibly valuable to be able to tell someone when they've hurt your feelings, misunderstood or generally made a bit of a mess of something.

In a type of therapy called mentalization-based treatment (MBT) this is made very explicit, with the therapist expecting to get things wrong and asking the client to tell them when they do.[4] MBT starts from the perspective that it's impossible for us to know what is in each other's minds, and the recognition that it can be painful to feel misunderstood. Practitioners in MBT work hard to make sure they are not guessing what someone else is feeling or incorrectly interpreting their actions. So, therapists frequently check in to be sure they understand what the client is meaning and also that the client is understanding the intended meaning of what the therapist is trying to convey.

It can feel tough to do this in a friendship. How often does someone miss the mark and hurt our feelings and yet we tell everyone else except them about it? Sometimes this is fine; we get over a small slight and give ourselves a bit of space from the friendship and come back to it with renewed appreciation for the person once we've let things simmer down. Other times it can lead to friendships gradually withering on the vine, and a sense that we should let the friendship go. How do we know which approach to take?

One helpful clue might be how that friendship makes us feel. If we are consistently spending time with someone who makes us feel less happy or less confident, then maybe it's a friendship in which our needs have fallen out of sync in some way. Perhaps our mutual needs aren't being met and maybe it's OK to hold this friendship more loosely. Friendships can cycle through periods of greater or less intensity, depending on what is going on for the friends at the time. Similar experiences can bring us closer together, and different phases of life might mean we fall out of step for a while. It doesn't mean the friendship is necessarily lost, but sometimes it can wax and wane over seasons. In these times I think it can help to have the idea of holding the relationship lightly. Rather than seeing it as an all-or-nothing binary, perhaps it's more like the tide, drawing away and coming back at its own pace. Sometimes it might not come back with the same intensity as before. We might outgrow relationships or recognize that we are seeking out familiar yet unhelpful patterns of interacting that we want to change.

It's painful, of course, to be on the reverse end of that – if you get the sense that a friend you are holding dear is finding the relationship less fulfilling for some reason. And it's hard to know what to do in that situation. Trying to talk about it definitely has its merits: there might be something you don't know about that is affecting the warmth or lack of it that you're feeling. Sometimes someone might have their own reason for withdrawing from a relationship, and there's not always anything we can do about that, except to try to be grateful for the relationship that was and hopeful for other friendships down the road.

One way of talking about it might be taking a leaf out the MBT book and trying to explicitly explain what we mean or what we have understood. In the aftermath of rows or awkward exchanges this can be especially useful. Once things have simmered down, revisiting the conversation and clearly outlining what it was that upset us and how we experienced something can help the other person understand why we got so tetchy. Similarly, asking what it was that upset the other person can be helpful if we are able to be open enough to hear it.

Starting from the point of view that both of us may have interpreted words or actions in a different way to how they were intended is a useful place to begin. These sorts of conversations are maybe easier to have with older friends and family members, but even with new friends they can reap rewards.

Making friends in general can feel more awkward as time goes on, but the same basic principles apply as for when children are establishing new relationships. Shared interests and proximity can aid new friendships, and being kind, and taking care with our conversations, rather than risking a joke at someone else's expense, can go a long way. Taking the time and energy to meet up and engage in mutual experiences is important; and also, possibly counter-intuitively, asking for help. Reciprocal asking for help with problems or with practical things can build relationships and indicate trust, so as long as it's not too one-sided, it can be a good thing to do.

In the light and heat of the summer months, I wonder if the promise of a new party, and a new person we might meet there, is also the promise of the opportunity to be a fresh version of ourselves: sparklier, more interesting, more charming... Of course with all relationships, whether friendships or romantic entwinements, *we* are the common factor, and we will always end up face to face with ourselves at some point within them.

With this in mind, as much as we may want to be whisked off our feet and dance all night, it might help to keep returning to ourselves to check in with how we are both physically and mentally. It's easy to forget to look after ourselves, to eschew making sure we're eating healthily enough and getting enough rest, but neglecting this can leave us fractious or emotionally volatile.

It's easy, too, to forget to notice how we're talking to ourselves in amongst the way we're talking to others, but remembering what we thought about in April's chapter on how to speak to ourselves kindly can give us a more helpful inner monologue. Being in a social whirlwind certainly doesn't mean that our own self-critical thoughts simmer down, and especially if hangovers or over-tiredness are in the mix.

Ideally, we will be able to balance being able to hold some attention on the outside world, on what people are *really* saying or doing, so that we don't overthink things in our own head, and also to have some attention on looking after ourselves in all ways. By balancing the energy we put both into friendships with others and our relationship with ourselves, we hopefully can feel a good connection with both.

FEELING CONNECTED

Key Ideas

1. If you feel yourself experiencing social anxiety remember that it's really common. Shifting your focus from yourself to others can help you escape the anxious thinking loops that it brings on. Try to look for evidence that people are enjoying what you say instead of evidence they aren't, and remember someone's listening face isn't always rapt attention.

2. Try to spot repeating patterns in your relationships, both helpful and unhelpful. If there are loops in relating that you repeatedly get into and that you want to change, think about what small actions you can do to step out of the usual dynamic or to alter the common thoughts you have, and think about who you can recruit to help you work out whether you're doing this.

3. Remember that no one can read your mind and you can't read anyone else's mind either. Experiment with explicitly saying what you mean and asking what someone else means. The more you do this the easier it gets.

4. Making new friends can feel hard, but consistently putting in the effort to have shared experiences and to both ask for help and offer it will often reap relationships.

5. It might feel boring, but remember that the physical effects of nights on the town can have a knock-on effect mentally. You might need to consciously make time for nourishment and rest in amongst socializing in order to get the most out of it. If you want some ideas about ways to rest, skip ahead to November's chapter on it: we need rest in any month.

6. Take care of how you speak to yourself too, as we thought about in April's chapter. It's hard to feel open and engaged if you are having a go at yourself. Try being kind instead, maybe even treating yourself to a date with yourself where you do something you really want to do.

7. If you were interested in the ideas on attachment theory, there is more on this in my book *Blueprint: How Our Childhood Makes Us Who We Are*. It doesn't suggest that everything is set in stone, but it goes through lots of juicy ideas about child development and how it influences us later on. You might also be interested in the book *Why Love Matters* by Sue Gerhardt, which goes into some of the neuroscience of attachment.

8. If you want further reading on social anxiety, *Overcoming Social Anxiety* by Gillian Butler is a good self-help guide to CBT for this problem.

7

JULY

3 a.m. Worries

Coping with Uncertainty and Existential Angst

t's not always personal things that cause us great anxiety. Sometimes the things that cause us concern are out in the world. July has always been a hotter month in the UK, but in recent years the heat of the summer months has ramped right up, as it has in many other countries. Writing this book, climate change has been on my mind, as I think about the different months of the year and the patterns of the seasons which we see unfold again and again. More and more the expected weather that a certain month is traditionally associated with is less easy to predict. Blossom creeping out in midwinter, leaves falling in summer, unexpectedly intense heatwaves, rainfall that causes flooding, changes in the timing of bird migration... we are changing the cycles of the planet we live on. The way we try to meet our needs impacts on the other species we share our planet with, and ultimately on our own too. The impact of human life on the planet we inhabit, and on each other, is by no means always positive, and the consequences can feel bleak.

My friend Chris and I have a 3 a.m. club. We both tend to wake up with worries at that time of the morning, and we are no stranger to those spirals of thought which seem so real in the dark early hours, but which by sunrise feel much less likely. The things I worry about in the middle of the night are often negligible, but we've all had plenty of existential threats in the last few years (big things that actually threaten our existence) – the climate emergency, the Covid-19 pandemic – on top of the usual existential dread which can appear for no real reason in the early hours (worrying that there is no point to anything, or that you can't locate your own sense of meaning for your life). The good news is that there are things we can do to manage existential dread. Even when the existential panic we are experiencing is about a real existential problem, there are still some things that can help. We might know that it's reasonable to feel scared, but that shouldn't stop us from being able to cope with the threat in the best possible way.

We all faced a big threat from 2020 onwards, when coronavirus emerged as a danger worldwide. Researchers measuring the effects of the pandemic in real time found, unsurprisingly, that levels of self-reported anxiety and low mood increased in the general population, and that specific groups had even more adverse effects: frontline staff experienced traumatic reactions to the situations they were regularly facing, vulnerable groups experienced higher levels of anxiety, and people with pre-existing mental health problems saw these exacerbated, with services stretched and not as present to help.[1,2] Children and young people experienced a sudden loss of their social milieu, and online environments became even more important.[3]

It will take a while to know what the impact of the pandemic will be on different groups and different generations, although it's clear that inequalities which were present before were amplified by the pandemic and few countries managed to design a policy which levelled this out (the UK certainly didn't). We are still stepping through the effects and understanding what may have changed, internally as well as externally, but some of the research we can learn from has been ongoing already, pre-pandemic.

The pandemic meant we were all suddenly living with a great deal of uncertainty about what exactly was going on, where the dangers were and what we should be doing about it. When different measures did come in we had no idea how long these would last. I remember those first few weeks of hand-washing so much that my hands got sore, of not being sure how careful we should be of shopping being brought into the house, and of that initial lockdown when the streets fell silent and none of us knew how long it was going to be for. We had to tolerate not knowing, and that is hard.

Psychologists have been researching how we tolerate uncertainty for some time pre-pandemic. Uncertainty faces us all the time in life: we don't know what's going to happen next, even though it feels like we do. We don't know when we will get sick, or die, or win the lottery, or fall in love... we can't plan these things. I sometimes even like that feeling: that you could walk past a house where one day you could conceivably end up living, and that each year we live through days which will one day have more meaning to us: an anniversary of a relationship we haven't yet started; or, even bigger, the date of birth, or death, of a loved one. Day to day we tend not to sit and contemplate all of this, though. Instead, we usually carry on fairly obliviously, thinking that one day is likely to be much the same as the one before it, because often it is.

Except when it isn't. Existential crises can happen in all phases of life. They can be global threats like climate change or pandemics, or more personal crises: break-ups, job nightmares, or health problems. Everyone finds uncertainty difficult, but to greater or lesser degrees people can come to tolerate it. Whether or not we can tolerate uncertainty isn't a fixed personality trait; it gets influenced by other things that are going on in our lives. When different things happen our ability to cope with the unknownness of things changes.

One of the things which impacts on how well we can tolerate uncertainty is how much we have at stake at the time, and this is one way in which either global or personal existential crises can intersect with the other vulnerabilities we have in our lives and create inequalities. In the pandemic, for example, people who were more financially at risk experienced more stress and were more at risk of coping poorly with uncertainty, whereas people with a financial cushion may have still felt stressed but not to the same degree. Understandably, if we know we have more to risk, then we'll feel more scared.

Overall, research has found that intolerance of uncertainty has been increasing in all of us since the 1990s.[4]

One hypothesis about the reason behind this is that it is related to the extent to which people have access to the internet and mobile phones. From the 1990s to now there has been a huge step change in the amount of connected-ness we experience and the access to information which we all have. Perhaps one side effect of having access to more information and at all times of day or night, via the inter-net, means that we feel less certain about things, or less able to tolerate feeling uncertain. Too much information can sometimes be unhelpful: it can either feel overwhelm-ing to have too much and not know what to believe, or it can mean that in situations where it simply isn't possible to know something, we're no longer used to tolerating that not-knowingness.

On a small, personal level this makes me think of how I used to make arrangements in the time before we all had a mobile phone. We used to plan to meet somewhere and then if someone didn't turn up, we'd wait for them. We might, at a push, use a phonebook to call someone's house, but if they didn't arrive, we had to either wait some more or go on our way, without knowing what had happened until we heard from them or saw them later. Now, we all have a direct line in our pocket, to let someone know we're running late or to ask someone if they're OK and if they're still coming. Which is very convenient, but maybe we're a bit less able to sit and wait and not know as a result. It's helpful to recognize that our tolerance for uncertainty has changed over time, because it suggested to the psycholo-gists that there might be some elements of intolerance of uncertainty which we have some control over: some things that we end up doing as a result which can get us into a vicious cycle that makes the uncertainty feel worse.[5]

In the height of the coronavirus pandemic, I certainly felt very intolerant of uncertainty. In those first mad weeks there was 24/7 coverage of all things coronavirus, and yet also a lot of unknowns... How did it spread? Who was most at risk? What precautions should we be taking? The not-knowing felt frightening.

During the first UK lockdown I interviewed Professor Mark Freeston,[6] a researcher who has spent much of his career studying how we cope with uncertainty (we met him very briefly in January's chapter when we were thinking about decision-making). Mark Freeston has spoken to many people who have been affected by dementia, the progression of which is very unknowable and also very threatening, as well as people affected by other chronic and fluctuating illnesses. Some of the things he has learnt from how people cope with this enabled him to advise on what might help any of us cope with any uncertainty, including what I was experiencing in the first lockdown.

Mark Freeston categorized information into three different types: information we need to know, information that might be interesting to know and information that is unhelpful or counterproductive. So during the peak of Covid-19 we might have needed to know what the rules were that we had to follow, and we might have been interested in knowing the answers to questions about how society was managing the pandemic, and then we might have found unreliable or even malicious information much less helpful. Even the interesting information might be unhelpful in the sense that it might be unknowable, and generate more uncertainty. In other situations, the same categories often apply.

There are other times in our lives when we might be tolerating huge uncertainty. Mark Freeston has emigrated three times in his life: from the UK to New Zealand, then to Quebec and then back to the UK. Each time he had to face uncertainty about what to expect, about what his new life was going to be like. Similarly, he highlighted experiences such as moving in with a new partner and having a baby as times of big change and great uncertainty. We might want to know how it is going to be, but ultimately it's unknowable.

This made me think about several times of change in my own life, including that move to Bristol – it wasn't an emigration but the same unknowingness was there. During the later coronavirus lockdowns I was also pregnant, and this was another strange and liminal time: I read so many books about birth, but ultimately the experience I had was impossible to plan for. And it's uncomfortable, to be in a state of uncertainty: it's deeply vulnerable. The unknowableness of what is to come in life is suddenly much more obvious.

So what can we do? Especially at times when our consciousness about this uncertainty is highlighted? Mark Freeston's research identifies two things. The first is that it helps to really manage our information diet. Where are we getting our information from and is it helpful or not? Not only news sources and how reliable they are, but information closer to home too. Are the birds still singing near us?

What are some of the things that we or other people are doing to help others out? This can make it easier for us to manage big global existential events such as pandemics and wars and the effects of the climate crisis too: what local information can we keep track of to help us feel anchored and as if we're making a meaningful difference? We can be selective about our news intake instead of doom-scrolling or having the news on in the background all the time. This doesn't mean ignoring what's going on out there, but it does mean actively selecting which programmes we watch or listen to and which articles we read, instead of having a wallpaper of news the entire time.

The second thing that can help is actively looking for information which balances things out. The news gives us information about threat, usually. We also need signals that we are safe: not just an absence of threat but something which communicates a presence of safety. It doesn't mean reassurance that nothing bad will ever happen – that's impossible – but small signs that things are OK at the moment. So, keep reassuring routines the same, for example, whether that is going for a walk, or having a cup of tea in a favourite mug, or making sure you do the recycling. What are the routines that help us to feel settled and safe and how can we keep doing them? This then helps our perception of threat to reduce and our anxiety to go down, which in turn helps us to process the information we do take in a bit more constructively.

It's worth being aware, too, that it's not only external signals of threat which can create feelings of anxiety. It might also be internal signals, or resonances with previous difficult experiences. So individuals who have already experienced trauma or adversity might be extra-sensitive to feeling anxious in the face of uncertainty. This makes total sense: we tend to learn from past experiences and we might be more on high alert if we've got a backdrop of having to manage a threatening situation before. The same things can still be helpful, though – trying to create routines that help us to feel safe and manage our information diet so we aren't overwhelmed.

Flipping this advice on its head tells us what is unhelpful too. Being less selective about our information diet, and trying to read every possible thing to prevent uncertainty, is one thing that can make us feel worse. This is especially true if it's an unknowable problem – we don't know what will happen in pandemics or climate crises, any more than we know how a birth will go or how we will feel once we've moved far away. In some ways, trying to read everything there is to read about a worry can be seen as what psychology refers to as a safety behaviour – something we do to try and keep anxiety at bay, but which can end up making it worse. There are plenty of coping strategies we all use that can accidentally make anxiety feel more prominent, from more severe examples like self-harm or over-controlled eating, to more innocuous examples like carrying multiple bottles of antibac just in case we lose one when we are out and about. It's hugely tempting to try to research your way out of an existential worry (the amount of books I had about birth is surely testament to that), but at some point this tends to tip from giving us helpful information to making us feel frantic in our quest for an impossible answer to a question which we can't know yet: what is going to happen next?

We can use these approaches in lots of different situations where uncertainty is around. Let's think about Esme. She has been working in a demanding job for some years, responsible for a school which is due to be inspected by Ofsted, the education body. She has become consumed with worry about the outcome of the report. This began by being motivational – it helped her rally the staff team to prepare – but Esme has no control over when the visit will be, or over several components of the inspection. She finds herself working out who the inspectors are likely to speak to, what time of day they are likely to come – things that she actually can't possibly know. She reads reports for so many other schools to try to get clues and tips that they all start blending into one. She skips lunch to work on planning and cancels her out-of-work plans so she can spend more time reading websites where other headteachers discuss how they managed Ofsted inspections. The worry is stopping her sleeping and making her miserable and she knows this could go on for weeks.

With support, Esme takes steps to tackle some of the things which are not productive. She realizes that reading all the extra information has got to a point which is unhelpful. She has prepared as best she can and she is doing the best she can at her job anyway, even without an inspection saying this. She stops reading the websites and the other reports and makes time to have a proper lunchbreak and to start doing some of her outside interests again. She finds the familiar routines help her to feel a bit more relaxed, and this helps her respond better to difficulties as they arise within the school day. On the day the inspectors do arrive, Esme is in the middle of dealing with a tricky issue, but continues what she's doing instead of dropping everything. She is praised by the inspectors for the way she manages this, and the report is good enough, despite some areas for improvement. Esme gets through these difficult few days, but more importantly, she has realized beforehand that there is a limit to how much she can control how the whole thing goes.

Uncertainty is tiring, and so is worrying, so worrying about uncertainty is a double whammy. Life is difficult sometimes. We do face existential messes as we share the planet with each other, and living (and dying) can bring us face to face with big dilemmas. Everyone is bad at tolerating this to some degree but at least we know from the research that there are some things that can help, in particular staying in the moment with our search for safe routines that anchor us and controlling how we use the information available to us. In some ways this is sifting through to find things that we can control in amongst the chaos of things we can't (which we will come back to again in September's chapter about work).

Another existential threat which we are all facing, and which is very real, is the damage that we are doing to the Earth, and the climate crisis which is resulting. Worries about this have understandably been escalating, along with warnings about how serious it is, and it's something which the young people I've seen for therapy in the last few years have been more and more concerned about.

Eco-anxiety isn't an official diagnosis, but it's been used by the American Psychological Association (APA) in a report about the effects of climate change. The climate emergency is a real problem which we should all be worrying about, but if these worries create significant distress, it might stop us from being able to get on both with our day-to-day lives and our ability to act to mitigate climate change on a personal level, and that's when the term eco-anxiety might be used.

Although some degree of unease might motivate us to do what we can to help slow climate change, if eco-anxiety is feeling unmanageable we can draw upon the same ideas which help us to tolerate uncertainty, and also some ideas from other treatments for anxiety. Just like with the worries about the pandemic that we thought about earlier, being careful about how we search for information is a good way to go. Choosing to look for information from reputable sources, and in a conscious, targeted way, rather than having a 24/7 spool of news unravelling about how doomed we all are, for example. We might also try to make sure that we balance time spent thinking about climate change and big existential problems, with spending time doing other things that interest us, including staying connected with people we care about. It doesn't make us any more helpful to scare ourselves the whole time about what is potentially going to happen next; indeed it probably makes us less helpful. Trying to keep our day-to-day present-moment sense of safety can enable us to feel calm enough to then take positive action. Separating out the things we can control and that we can't control, and choosing to do those controllable things and remind ourselves that we are doing them, can then help us to feel a sense of agency. So we can decide to eat less meat, cut out flying, and join an activist group, for example, and do what actions we can on a daily basis that contribute to reducing the problem rather than exacerbating it. The anxiety we feel might help to spur us on, if we can use it in this way.[7]

Paying attention to how we think about big problems like climate change can also help: are we getting into those catastrophizing loops of thinking where everything feels pointless or can we focus on the positive things we can do to prevent our anxiety spiralling out of control? Sometimes breaking such a huge problem down into smaller components to consider or take action on can be helpful in getting us unstuck when we feel overwhelmed, instead of getting stuck in that rumination that we thought about in January's chapter, where we chew over and over stuff that has already happened and that we can't change.

Some of what we can control is boringly obvious, but just because something is obvious doesn't mean that it's any more likely we will do it. I spent years advising people I saw for therapy to cut down on caffeine if they felt anxious, while I was merrily drinking upwards of seven cups of tea and coffee a day. I really noticed when I finally cut this down myself, just how nice it is not to have a background state of feeling slightly jittery. Similarly, making the time to eat better and get as much sleep as possible can have a massive impact on our mood. It's not particularly groundbreaking but it is so good for our health, both physical and mental, and it can take the level of worry we experience down a notch or two, and make us less reactive to potential worries in the moment.

For all we can control these things, there is much we can't control. While we can plan for the worst and hope for the best, in the end things unfold as they unfold and we can't be responsible for all of it. At this point it can help to think about some of what we considered in April's chapter: how we hold ourselves in all of this. Life is messy, and it can be painful, so how do we treat ourselves with the kindness we would show a dear friend in the midst of all we are trying to deal with? If I am feeling anxious about what is to happen next, what can I do to make things just one tiny bit easier for myself? How can I make myself even 1 per cent more comfortable? Is it a pause for a deep breath? Is it reminding myself I am doing the best I can? Is it stopping to acknowledge that I am experiencing suffering to some degree, and that I send myself love and kindness and hope for myself to be free from pain? Just as Mark Freeston noticed that the small things can make a big difference to our sense of safety, so small actions and words directed towards ourselves can help us weather difficult storms that rage around us. Just like the weather, as unpredictable as that is now, we can be sure that our thoughts and feelings will shift and change as time goes on. Worries might still remain but we will hold them more or less tightly at different times. Even the things that we can't change – regrets and losses and difficult memories – we might make space for in a different way (more on this in October's chapter on loss).

For what it's worth, even though I haven't met you, I am wishing you freedom from suffering too. We are all living through uncertainties and stresses, and you are doing the best you can with the information you have to hand. If things feel hard sometimes, if you feel you have made mistakes or not done enough to tackle the existential worries at hand, you are not alone in that. And if something is anxiety-provoking that doesn't mean you're doing the wrong thing. Just keep going, and know that we are all in this messy old business together, and we are all on this rock of a planet, breathing in, breathing out, and trying the best we can to muddle through.

COPING WITH UNCERTAINTY AND EXISTENTIAL ANGST

Key Ideas

1. Tolerating uncertainty is hard. It's human. And some things in life are difficult.

2. It can help to manage your information diet: select information which is reliable and useful, and limit doom-scrolling or endless research into unanswerable questions.

3. We don't just need an absence of threat, we also need the presence of safety. Encourage yours by making time for small things that give you a sense of safety, and trying to notice small things in the here and now which show you things are OK.

4. Sift through what is in your control and not. Do what you can and then remind yourself of what you are doing. Make some of what you do about looking after yourself physically: sleep, less caffeine, good food, all make a difference to how you feel.

5. If your worries are about something specific, like the climate emergency, then think of what small actions you can do which will be helpful and start with them.

6. Hold yourself gently in the uncertainties of life. Think of what will make you feel 1 per cent more

comfortable, and speak to yourself with the kindness that you would speak to a loved one.

7. This is a slightly random recommendation, but the Dr Seuss book (for children) called *Oh! The Places You'll Go!* is a really nice one for capturing the sense of life's uncertain adventure.

8

AUGUST

Hot Under the Collar

Managing Anger

August in the UK is one of the hottest months. Hot, sticky days and airless, sleep-starved nights can make the heat seem inescapable and can fray our nerves. Even in the sun-poor UK, where a mere sliver of sun causes people to strip off and sunbathe near-naked in the park, a summer heatwave can feel like too much of a good thing.

Anger also feels hot. Whether it's bubbling away under the surface, a seething pool of resentment getting ready to be unleashed, or erupting in a firework display of hurtful words and cross faces, it's not chance that we talk about needing to 'cool down' after a row, or to 'take the heat out' of a situation.

It turns out all these heat-based metaphors fit well with the research on anger and hot weather. Hotter climates are associated with increased levels of anger and aggression. A whole range of studies have looked at the association, and when researcher Craig Anderson reviewed these in 1989[1] he found impressive correlations between heat and peaks in violent crimes (although December also had more murders, which could be an effect of Christmas: when domestic violence sadly tends to escalate during the perfect storm of increased financial pressures, increased alcohol consumption and a greater likelihood of being cooped up together).

Craig Anderson's analysis found that hotter regions of the world, hotter years, hotter quarters of years, hotter seasons, months and even days all correlate with relatively more aggressive behaviours including murder, assault, riot and domestic violence. In 1997 he and his colleagues looked again at how shifts in temperature year-to-year relate to violent crime and property crime in the US.[2] They found hotter temperatures were associated with violent crime (but not property crime), even after several other factors were allowed for (such as poverty and population age effects). They also found that the magnitude of the increase in violent crime over summer was related to the number of hot days in that period, suggesting it is the heat which is responsible, not another factor related to summer holidays. So if we're more likely to be feeling a bit irritable at this time of year, perhaps it's worth us spending some time with anger.

It's easy to feel like anger is a negative emotion, something that needs to be solved or squashed. When young people I've worked with are referred for 'anger management' it's usually because an adult in their lives is finding their anger a problem, rather than the young person themselves. Should we always try to be squashing anger, though? And is it always a bad thing?

Anger can be energizing. Just like anxiety in the previous chapter can motivate us to do things differently, so rage at how things shouldn't be can get us motivated to change a situation, as long as we can channel that anger constructively. If instead of lashing out hurtfully or turning our anger in on ourselves, we can use it to do something productive – to speak up, to influence things for the better – then often we end up feeling better as well as getting something helpful done. Channelling anger also takes us out of the trap of snapping at others, then feeling bad about ourselves, then snapping even more.

Anger can be hard to harness in this way, though, especially for anyone in a minority position who is challenging the status quo. It's not easy to have logical and constructive conversations about something which feels too personally threatening, and usually requires the support of others to enable us to feel emotionally safe enough to channel anger effectively.

Nonetheless, anger can be a helpful signpost. There's usually a reason for it. Sometimes that's an injustice; sometimes it's a situation which is untenable or an unreasonable demand; sometimes it's actually a cover for another emotion, like sadness or worry. If we take the time to tease things apart a little, we can often find valuable clues which can help us to know what feelings or circumstances we need to be acting on.

In the intense environment of inpatient mental health wards where I've worked, angry outbursts can happen quite suddenly. On occasions when I've been involved in trying to help a young person and a staff team make sense of what has brought about a flashpoint of aggression or violence, there has always been a reason for it. Sometimes it's to do with frustration or a sense of injustice, but very often it's been to do with a sense of threat. The young person who ends up threatening the people around them has first of all felt under threat themselves. I've felt threatened myself on very rare occasions. I remember a young person slamming themselves against a door I was on the other side of and calling me all sorts of things, shouting into my face through the glass window in the door which exited the ward into the staff corridor and leaving me feeling frightened to go into work the next day. Talking things through afterwards with the young person involved, it was clear that this was a very effective communication of how they were feeling at the time: unsafe, out of control, at a loss of what to do, scared, vulnerable, and yes angry too, at a system that felt unhelpful, or perhaps even harmful.

It's not only patients on mental health wards that get involved in this sort of acting out in a clinical setting; it's also the staff, sometimes hampered by working conditions, or feeling frustrated by a sense of a lack of progress, or feeling angry on young people's behalf. Sometimes it's hard to pinpoint what anger or frustration is about, but different ways of seeing a problem within the staff team can give rise to disagreements too, although angry outbursts hopefully stay contained within structures of meetings and reflective practice sessions, where they can be usefully explored and understood.

Whoever it is that is feeling things that are so large that they are uncontainable, being able to name the feelings they are experiencing, whether anger or something else, is half the battle. When we don't know what we feel we can lash out without thinking, and we often make things worse. Children's books like *Barbara Throws a Wobbler* and *The Bad-Tempered Ladybird* tend to capture these helpful ideas: the former in particular enabling children to recognize and name their feelings and see them as separate from themselves. They themselves are not their bad mood, they are experiencing a bad mood, and this too will pass. Finding a way to recognize what we feel and how we are reacting to it sounds obvious but can be really powerful.

Let's think of John, a young man who feels a lot of understandable anger towards his family, who struggle to meet his needs for emotional closeness and support. John's family don't engage in conversations when he tries to highlight what he needs, leaving him feeling like he is the one being unreasonable. Left alone with his emotions and unmet needs his thoughts quickly become self-critical and spiral, attacking himself for all sorts of things – how he feels, how he behaves, how unlovable he must be for people to keep ignoring him in the way they do. To manage the feelings that these thoughts bring up he uses a range of coping strategies, from starting rows about small things and shouting at other people close to him, to more obviously self-destructive behaviours like punching walls or getting into fights which it's obvious he will lose.

John's anger is a real response to an emotionally painful situation. The therapeutic work John can do is not to squash or deny that he is angry, but to recognize other emotions that are also lurking, like deep sadness, and fear of being alone, and then to spot unhelpful patterns that he is using to manage those feelings but which make things worse. For John, rows and self-harm felt helpful to some extent in the past as a way of letting off steam, but he begins to recognize that they are no longer serving him well. He feels stuck in a pattern that leads to people around him being pushed further away, and him feeling even more alone.

Teasing apart what is going on, and then practising some different reactions, sounds simple but takes effort and hard work. In time, though, and using individual therapy, John begins doing things differently: not always, but more often than not. He pauses more before shouting, he takes time to work out what he wants to say, and he sees more clearly that some responsibility for what happens in relationships lies with his family and with the friends around him as well as with John himself. John works on talking to himself as he would a good friend and on learning some ways of soothing himself so that things don't go so fast from nought to a hundred. He tries to spend time with people who made him feel supported. He doesn't stop feeling angry, but he understands it more, acknowledges it more and increasingly knows how to work with it.

If we can harness it, anger can be useful, but it can also often lead to problems in relationships or unhelpful destructive behaviours. It's not the emotion itself that is the problem, but the things it can end up getting us doing or saying. Learning how best to grapple with anger can pay dividends, and several types of therapy have some interesting takes on this.

One school of thought which handles anger wisely is dialectical behaviour therapy (DBT).[3] DBT was created to help with the extreme ups and downs in mood which come with chronic exposure to trauma, but the approach has been tested for other problems too, including difficulties with anger. A dialectic is a deep-rooted contradiction, and at the therapy's heart is the idea that both acceptance and change are necessary, even though they feel in opposition. It's important to accept who we are now and how things have been as well as striving for positive change. I think of a dialectic as an impossible dilemma, such as 'It is impossible for me to stop self-harming' and 'I need to stop self-harming.'

In relation to anger, this means it's useful to accept that we are feeling angry, possibly for several good reasons, at the same time as trying to do something more constructive with the emotion. Like many therapeutic ideas this sounds great but can be really hard to put into practice in the day to day, especially if we are seething with bottled-up rage. This bottling up of rage is often what happens when we don't accept our feelings. Anger pent up is like a wasp trapped in a bottle... it's not going to end well when it gets let out.

DBT teaches a range of skills, based on four key areas: emotional regulation, distress tolerance, mindfulness, and interpersonal effectiveness.

Emotion regulation coaches people to appreciate all emotions as having value of some kind that can be harnessed, and it tries to help people recognize and name the emotion instead of squashing it, and to 'ride the wave' of a big feeling rather than react impulsively and unhelpfully. This riding the wave sounds like the stuff of motivational posters, but how can it actually be worked on?

One exercise that DBT suggests harnesses the principle of opposite action. It is what it says on the tin: whatever we're tempted to do, we should do the opposite. So if we're furious and we want to shout, we could instead make the effort to speak really softly and carefully. If our anger is making us want to push people away, we could try approaching people and being kind instead.

Although doing the exact opposite isn't always appropriate, the basic principle of this is strong, and you can adapt the extent to which you oppose feelings according to the situation at hand. It depends who you're angry with and why, but it's an interesting idea to throw into the mix and sometimes it does pay dividends. Making your partner or friend a cup of tea when you're feeling really hacked off instead of having a go might open up new possibilities for dialogue. On the other hand, if you're justifiably angry with an injustice at work being nice about it might not always feel like an acceptable course of action: in that case aiming for being professional and thinking about how to constructively problem-solve might be a better path to take, and squashing anger entirely might just seep out as passive-aggression.

Another emotion regulation idea which borrows a lot from more traditional cognitive therapy is the idea of checking the facts. We might feel like everything is totally unfair and we have been unjustly treated by everyone, but what are the objective facts? Is there any evidence to the contrary? If we're searching for evidence to disprove what we're thinking instead of only things that back us up we can sometimes be surprised.

Principles of distress tolerance include the practices of radical acceptance and self-soothing. We'll think more about radical acceptance in December's chapter, but basically it's the idea that even if something totally awful has happened, we work to accept that reality rather than causing ourselves more pain by constantly pushing it away. It doesn't mean we have to forgive people who have caused massive pain, or accept the situation thinking that it's OK that something bad has happened. But we can think something shouldn't have happened and at the same time acknowledge that it did. Sometimes people are struggling to accept huge life-changing events which have been foisted on them entirely unfairly, and it's not to say that circumstances or people are forgiven if radical acceptance is being employed. It does mean that the struggle around the 'if only this hadn't happened' becomes less, though.

Self-soothing is another practice from distress tolerance, and involves using all our senses to try to calm ourselves down. What soothes me might not be what soothes you, but if we both have a list of things that work for us then we can pull them out of the bag when we need them. Some people are soothed by chilled-out music, others find death metal soothing; it's whatever works.

Mindfulness is the act of staying in the present moment, instead of getting caught up in thoughts about the past or the future. Like many useful therapeutic techniques, mindfulness is also a bit of a victim of its own success, with so many books, audio recordings and courses available that it sometimes gets referred to as McMindfulness.

Nonetheless, done well I think it is one of the most helpful therapeutic skills I use, and I notice it when I consistently try to practise it myself. The more I do it the more time I have between feeling an emotion and acting on it – a brief pause before reacting which means I can respond slightly more intentionally. Deceptively simple-sounding, it's actually really hard to keep our attention trained on what is happening right now. The phrase 'monkey mind' comes from the tendency we all have to jump our attention from one thing to another, all too rarely really noticing where we are right now.

Mindfulness is a practice, just like we practise any other skill we learn. The more I do it the more I notice the benefits of it, but of course we often need it most when we are stressed and overrun and find it hard to make the time for it.

The final DBT skill set is interpersonal effectiveness. This is basically about balancing one's own needs with the needs of others, but without trampling all over someone else to get what you want or negating what you need altogether. This involves assertiveness, which we thought about in May's chapter on talking and listening. Remember, this is the skill of not being passive or aggressive about what we want from other people, and also thinking about the relationships we have with others and how we view ourselves within those relationships. If we can't treat ourselves with kindness it's hard to attract or allow that same kindness from others. Talking to others when we're angry is a huge challenge. If we're virtually on a hair trigger it doesn't take much to push our buttons.

DBT suggests using several techniques to try to slow things down, keep calm and stay assertive rather than flipping into being aggressive. Lots of these tend to be summarized in acronyms, like FAST, which stands for be Fair, don't Apologize unless it's warranted, Stick to your values and be Truthful. By concentrating on ways to be fair and measured in conversations the idea is that it might help us not to flip between feeling like we are promoting someone else's needs over our own, or the reverse – stamping on someone else's needs in order to get ours met. Having something else to concentrate on as a guide to how we want to interact can be a helpful distraction if anger is building up, and can also help us to plan how we want to approach interactions, if we're aware that they might be tricky.

John, who we met earlier, uses these acronyms to remember some of the skills he has learnt in the moment when they might be useful. He has a bad start to the day: he wakes up to an answerphone message from his brother which puts him in a really foul mood first thing, stirring up feelings of sadness and inequality and anger. He knocks over the milk at breakfast and it goes everywhere, and he's late getting into work because of this. When his manager asks why he's late he is about to blow, when he stops, looks out the window for a minute and takes a really deep breath as he notices what he can see out there as a way to ground himself. He takes another deep breath and thinks about FAST. It's not fair to shout at his manager about him being late. It wasn't John's fault he was late, but an apology is warranted. He says sorry for not being on time and explains he had a nightmare start today. His manager appreciates the apology and the explanation, and suggests maybe waking slightly earlier in the mornings so there is time to accommodate things going wrong, because he really values having John there first thing. Then he offers to get John a coffee and John feels the trajectory of his day beginning to take a slight upturn, as he feels connected to his manager and pleased that he didn't blow his top.

DBT is by no means the only therapeutic approach with something to say about anger. All types of therapy have something to add to the mix, but another which I have often used with people is acceptance and commitment therapy (ACT). This is the same approach we met earlier on (in January and February) which prioritizes thinking about values. ACT harnesses mindfulness too, but with a slightly different emphasis to DBT. Key to ACT is the idea that we can be more *psychologically flexible* in our lives if we pay attention to thoughts and feelings as temporary inner states, like an internal weather system blowing through, and think about ourselves more like the sky in this metaphor, rather than the clouds or the rain. So we are not our angry thoughts and feelings, and we can choose to behave in ways which are still committed to our core values that we want to live by. Crucially, we accept that those feelings are there – we don't try to push them away, neither do we hop on them and act according to them.

Again, it sounds easy but it's actually really hard, yet practising seeing our thoughts and feelings as something that we can observe, and don't need to act on, can be one helpful step in coping with emotions that feel overwhelming or thoughts that seem to push our buttons and get us feeling het up. Even saying to ourselves, 'I'm having the thought that this is really unfair', 'I'm having the feeling that I'm really hurt by this person', can be useful in slightly separating ourselves from the whirlwind of thoughts and feelings that can whisk us up into a frenzy and lead to unkind behaviours.

Trying to keep our eye on the core values we want to embody can also be powerful. We're often encouraged to think about the goals that we want to reach. As we discussed before, thinking about values is different – we can't arrive at a value in the same way we can tick off a goal. I don't ever 'achieve kindness'. But I can try to bring kindness into the way I act in lots of different situations. Trying to create enough of a pause to think about how I might introduce kindness into a conversation, even if I'm feeling frustrated, can help to shift things slightly. Similarly with values such as prioritizing family – bringing this to mind in a tense conversation with a family member might encourage us to take a deep breath and speak a bit more softly or respectfully, and a little can go a long way.

ACT also encourages us to try to see other people with compassion, as other flawed humans just like us. This is super-hard if the human in question has done something that has wronged us, and it doesn't mean that we have to condone that behaviour, but being able to see them as more than a caricature of their bad behaviours can help us to let go of some of the frustration and anger that is unhelpful for us to carry around. As I'm writing this, I know that it is helpful to be able to approach previous wrongs with this attitude, and I also know that it's extremely hard, and that recommending such an approach can sound a bit annoying. Why should I forgive someone who is being unhelpful or even abusive? And no one has to do anything. But if we're harbouring an anger that begins to feel like it's gnawing at our very bones, then the person that forgiveness ends up helping is often ourselves.

I am lucky enough to have gone through my life without suffering the horrendous trauma which some of the people I have sat across from in therapy have, and I certainly wouldn't dream of telling someone to forgive someone else. On the other hand, in my own life, I have also seen the power of trying to use compassion to approach situations and people about whom I have felt intense anger. Times when I have been especially angry have often been because I have been hurt, or someone I love has been hurt, but when the hot feelings of anger have cooled down I can mostly see that it's not been a purposeful hurt on someone else's part. That doesn't necessarily make it easier – it still feels bad – but it does perhaps mean that there is a little more room for some softness towards the person or people who have been involved in that hurt. Sometimes they were hurt too, and lashing out, or sometimes they just weren't able at the time to do better, even though I might wish that they had been. Whether this applies to someone being obstructive or aggressive at work, someone falling short of what was hoped for in a relationship, or failings in what we reasonably expected from a service or organization, the same principles are often true: that nurturing anger, while occasionally energizing, often actually creates more bad feeling for us and makes us more sensitive to feeling wronged in other, more neutral situations.

In some ways this is a type of perspective shift: flipping to seeing things through the eyes of the other person and acknowledging that they may have had a different frame of reference to you. Things often feel bigger if we stew in them, ruminating on thoughts about how unfair something is or how wrong someone is. Taking a different perspective can also involve zooming out and trying to see what's going on from either far in the future or from far away. Literally, thinking about your life as one small part of the whole country, planet, solar system, can act to call up the sort of overview perspective that astronauts report feeling from space when they look back at the planet: they suddenly get a sense of how small we are and get a different sense of scale about our problems.[4] Again, I'm not saying that trying to view things from a removed perspective is always helpful if there's a real wrong which needs to be righted, and it's not helpful to quell anger that can be usefully directed into reducing inequality or righting a wrong, but for everyday furies there can be such a sense of relief from zooming up into space in your mind's eye and looking back down, or from zooming forward five years and asking yourself how much this will matter then.

Dominik Mischkowski and colleagues[5] set up an experiment to look at the effect of shifting our perspective, specifically trying to get some distance. In a series of experiments with students which were designed to irritate them during various tasks, they tested the effect of getting participants to recall the irritation from the first-person perspective or from the perspective of a fly on the wall. Taking the perspective of the fly was associated with less angry rumination and less aggressive behaviour. In the heat of the moment, trying to see the situation from someone else's point of view, even if that is one of a neutral observer (or a fly), seems to be helpful.

I love the saying, 'Don't just do something, sit there.' I don't know who coined it originally, but it chimes with mindfulness approaches described above, and fits with all sorts of behaviours that anger can tempt us into acting upon. Anger seems like one of the emotions that are most likely to coax us into being unreasonable and then regretting it.

Venting is one example of this. 'Having a vent' to 'get things off our chest' is something that often gets recommended, and when we're angry it's easy to feel like doing just that will help us to 'let off some steam', but the evidence suggests that this is likely to make us feel worse: angrier and more likely to act angrily too. Similar results have been found with the idea of physically letting off steam with a punchbag.

A neat experiment from the early 2000s by a researcher called Brad Bushman compared people's reactions after either thinking about the person they were angry with as they punched a punchbag, or thinking about getting fit as they punched a punchbag.[6] The research team also had a control group of people who didn't do anything: no punching and no thinking about anything specific. They found that distraction, by thinking about getting fit while punching the bag, worked better at reducing anger than ruminating over what they were angry about while punching the punchbag, but doing nothing at all was the best thing for reducing anger. People were also less aggressive if they hadn't been in the first two conditions (so they hadn't either thought about their anger or punched anything) as measured by their likelihood to accept the opportunity to blast a loud noise at the person they were annoyed with. Putting aside the comic value of blasting a loud noise at someone, the experiment suggests that we can exacerbate anger by running over it in our minds, or by taking it out with our fists.

It's hard, though, just to let angry feelings slide. Instead it's all too easy to snap and niggle and get into a pattern that creates more anger within ourselves and the relationships we cultivate. Hurtful words are out of our mouths and slapped around the face of someone else before we've had the chance to think about the consequences and suck them in. Another way we can end up making things worse is denying that we feel anger in the first place. How often have you felt really annoyed but tried to pick a fight with someone who has nothing to do with what you're annoyed about? Or have you ever tried to make the problem someone else's, telling them that they seem off when actually it's you who feels bad? I definitely do this.

The cliché of kicking the dog when we're upset with someone else, often ourselves, is a cliché for a reason. It's often easier to think about being annoyed with someone else than it is to acknowledge problems we might have with ourselves. Whether we call this projection (as psychodynamic theory does) or see it as a thinking style (as cognitive therapy might) or a family script that helps us through (as family therapy might), we sometimes know at some level that we're doing it. If we're lucky we'll work out what we're doing in time to apologize, or even stop it. Whatever we call it, it can be quite annoying for the person we are doing this to, and it can also prevent us from acknowledging and addressing our own feelings about something. It's hard to always notice that we're doing it, though – it's more likely someone else might point it out to us, which can also be annoying (but worth trying to listen to).

We don't always turn anger out on other people. We can also turn anger in on ourselves. This is sometimes what is happening when people engage in self-harming behaviours (which we will also think about in December's chapter). Self-harming behaviours of a whole range, from cutting to getting into fights that are unwinnable, can be an expression of anger turned inwards. I think sometimes we can be involved in aggressions towards ourselves on a smaller scale too: making choices that on some level we know are counterproductive, or unhelpful, or actively self-sabotaging. Of course these acts might not be to do with feeling any particular anger; we may have just got into a pattern of behaviour which we find it hard to escape from. Snapping at other people, or having a go at ourselves with an angry tone of voice: either way these repeated loops of behaviour can be worth examining and trying to break. Asking ourselves if the voice we are using towards ourselves is the one we would use for a good friend is a good starting point for this, as we thought about in April's chapter when we were looking at how we can talk to ourselves most helpfully.

It's not only the way we speak to ourselves that can have ripples of consequence, it's also the way we speak to and interact with others. The idea of modelling is an old theory from social psychology. A researcher called Albert Bandura devised a classic experiment with what he called 'bobo dolls', where he found that children who observe an adult hitting a doll were more likely to hit the doll themselves.[7] The bobo dolls were large, and round-bottomed, and they wobbled and then righted themselves after being hit (like a Weeble, if you're old enough to remember those). The behaviours we get into when we are angry are usually witnessed, and if we live with small children they are witnessed by some of the fastest learners around. This in itself can add layers of guilt and shame to the angry party, and make everything worse, so trying to pause and prevent ourselves from lashing out when we're angry is helpful for ourselves as well as those we might be lashing out at.

Trying to put a punctuation mark in *after* an angry interchange, and not feeling like the episode has to spiral off into a whole day of being in a terrible mood, is another thing that can work. Our bodies can sometimes help us do this – the good old 'count to ten and breathe deeply' advice, for example, is based on sound evidence. We can actually change our body's physiology by the way that we breathe.[8] Breathing out for longer than we're breathing in, for example, can help to soothe us, activating our parasympathetic nervous system, and making us feel calmer (more on this in November's chapter on rest).

So, while the heat of summer creates conditions which make us more likely to be irritable, our mood isn't only influenced by the heat and other environmental factors, but also by our internal context. As always, breathing, getting enough sleep, watching our nutrition, and making time for things that give us a sense of pleasure and achievement all help us to feel less depleted and more able to cope with the irritations of life with some grace. We can't always do much about all of these things, but the more we take care of the ones we can control the better we'll be able to manage the annoyances that come our way. Actively choosing to use some of the skills from DBT or ACT, to vent less, breathe more slowly and occasionally zoom out to have a fly-on-the-wall perspective can hopefully help to keep us from boiling over too often or too irreparably. And when we do... being kind to ourselves and trying to put a punctuation mark in the escalating spiral of angry mood and actions can be really useful, even though it's hard.

Anger isn't a bad thing in itself, but some of the things it gets us saying and doing can make us and the people around us feel pretty bad. Taking the time to try to control how we use it can give us a really helpful skill for all areas of our lives. It's probably hardest in these hot months, when irritation can sneak up on us and rise from mild annoyance to full-blown row quicker than we might like to admit. There are ways to try to manage this big emotion, though, and like many of the strategies and approaches in this book, the more we practise them the easier they are to have at our fingertips.

MANAGING ANGER

Key Ideas

1. It's helpful to see anger as part of the wide-ranging spectrum of feelings that we *all* have, which serve us well in all sorts of different ways. Instead of trying to squash it we can accept that we are feeling anger. This doesn't mean we have to act on it, though.

2. Sometimes anger is a mask for other painful feelings lurking underneath. Understanding what is underneath and then trying to address what that is can help dissolve the anger. This might mean tolerating sadness, taking practical steps to change something, or acknowledging the unfairness and possibly grief around a suboptimal situation. Ask yourself, is there only anger or is there something else? Any fear or sadness? Any worry or grief?

3. Anger can be useful. Is it a sign of something that would be helpful to change? Is there something you can do about it? What would be the smallest step towards making that change?

4. If you feel like you are getting stuck on angry thoughts or caught up in unhelpful angry behaviours, try to imagine how you would be if you were taking a moment to respond thoughtfully rather than reacting on autopilot. What would you like to be able to do? To take a breath in between feeling

angry and acting on that? To act in accordance with a particular value you hold dear?

5. If you're up for it, practising mindfulness when you're not angry can help you to pause when you are angry. It can help you catch yourself mid-flight in an emotion, or just before you step off the edge of the emotional trapeze platform. If you hate mindfulness you can still have a go at accepting the feeling but changing the action. You are the sky not the weather!

6. Watch out for angry tendencies to blame or identify anger in others which can be annoying. Are you always telling other people they seem angry when actually it's you?

7. Can you use DBT skills like assertiveness and self-soothing to help you practically manage anger which is destructive instead of constructive? Can you act the opposite? Or use a perspective-changing exercise like zooming out or zooming forward in time?

8. Don't forget your body. Breathing out for longer than in, making sure you are looking after yourself with sleep, good food and things you love, can have a surprisingly big effect on the buffer you have available to you to avoid angry blow-ups.

9. If you're interested in ACT, I'd recommend the book *ACTivate Your Life*, by Joe Oliver, Jon Hill and Eric Morris, and also *The Happiness Trap* and *The Confidence Gap*, both by Russ Harris.

10. If you're interested in DBT, then *The Dialectical Behavior Therapy Skills Workbook* by Matthew McKay might be helpful.

11. There is more on ACT, and other types of therapy (including CBT and DBT), in a podcast I made for the British Association for Behavioural and Cognitive Psychotherapies called Let's Talk About CBT which is available here: https://letstalk-aboutcbt.libsyn.com. It goes through different types of therapy which have CBT as their root, and also different types of problem for which CBT can be helpful.

9

SEPTEMBER

That Sunday Night Feeling

Making the Most of Work

September is back-to-school month. The smell of this time of year reminds me of new stationery and the mix of excitement and slight dread of going back to the classroom after a long break. As an adult I now feel this time mostly as a fresh start, an academic new year, even when I haven't been working principally in an academic setting. A sense of optimism in the slightly colder air.

As we grow up, school days are replaced by work days. We spend so much time at work that a lot of our dilemmas are based there. Work is a large part of who we are and how we live, and that's not necessarily a bad thing, but it means that how we feel at work can affect our mood elsewhere too. There's a lot that's known about how to be more contented in the workplace, some of which is to do with what the organization we work for does for us, and some of which is to do with how we use what is on offer.

As an adult many people tend to have some dread about work all year round. That Sunday night feeling that the fun is over and that we're back on the treadmill in the morning can prompt heartsink, especially when our jobs don't feel like they are fitting in the best way any more. A back-to-work panicky feeling doesn't always mean we're in the wrong job; sometimes it just means it's something new or outside of our comfort zone, which will stretch us and encourage us to grow. If we have it relentlessly and it feels heavier rather than exciting, then it might be that we're not in a job that is a good fit for us. Even that doesn't mean all is lost.

Thinking about which aspects of our work we have control over can be a helpful first step. We've touched on this before: trying to understand if a worry is something that we have some power over or if it is something which we cannot change, no matter how hard we try. Knowing the answer to this question is really useful. If we are spending all our time worrying about something that we just cannot do anything about, then that's wasted energy and it makes us feel helpless. If we try instead to change even the small things we do have some control over, then we are more likely to feel a sense of agency and achievement that can give us even more energy to tackle bigger things.

This isn't to say don't try to change the big stuff. Tackling systemic problems in the workplace is important too. But if we're trying to feel happier day to day, starting with a seemingly tiny thing can sometimes make a huge difference. I recommend mapping out two concentric circles (like a picture of a fried egg), an inner circle with room for things that are within your control and an outer one for things that are beyond your control. Sorting through the things that are getting you down at work, and putting them in one or the other ring, can illuminate subtle differences and help guide our actions. For example, I can't control a colleague's behaviour if she is consistently late to a meeting I chair. I can control what I choose to do about it. Do I stew silently or do I try to make time to explore with the colleague why they are always late? If I choose not to speak to them, then maybe I also need to try to let my annoyance go, because I'm opting out of doing what I can about it. This is also quite a nice example of how quite often, in true psychological style, it's a bit of this and a bit of that. Even for the stuff that we can't change, we can sometimes change how we think about it. I can choose to think my colleague doesn't value the meeting, or I can choose to remind myself of all the other things she is up against which might be making it hard to attend on time. I could even try to use the technique of zooming out which we thought about in August's chapter on anger: reminding myself that in the bigger scheme of things this is maybe not such a big deal.

This brings us neatly to locus of control. When I learnt about the idea of locus of control as an undergraduate I first heard it as locust of control. But there are no locusts here. Locus of control just means where it is that we perceive the control is over a situation. We tend to attribute the cause or control of events either to ourselves, or to something external to us. A fair amount of research[1] has gone into looking at the difference that an internal versus an external locus of control can have. When we think that things are within our control we are more likely to try to change them, and sometimes succeed. But, on the other hand, if things go wrong we might be more likely to blame ourselves. In a work context, feeling that we have more control is often motivational, but I do think it's worth doing the fried-egg diagram above to try to sift out what some of the quicker wins might be and focus energy there. Otherwise it can feel like banging your head on a brick wall and lead to feelings of burnout.

Thinking back to the experience of suddenly working from home that many of us had during the Covid-19 pandemic lockdowns is a potential source of times where we may have managed to take control. I remember the first couple of months of lockdown being endless Zoom meetings and urgent phone calls, as everyone tried to work out what we needed to be doing. Over time, things settled down a little and a bit more headspace was available to consider what was controllable about the new way of working. In the different places where I worked, we thought a lot about what the small things were that could make a big difference to staff morale. Things like going for a fake commute in the morning: a twenty-minute walk before the working day began, or making sure that tea breaks didn't get lost in the rush of trying to answer emails to prove that you were working. I had a Post-it note stuck to the wall by my desk which reminded me to leave the house, treat myself to nice tea or coffee, and stretch. I didn't manage to do these things every day, but the days I did definitely felt better.

The small actions we do every day can also add up to bigger shifts over time. If you're feeling unhappy at work it can be deflating and knock the energy out of you, especially if you've been applying for jobs for a while. Trying to find a project you can devote a small amount of time to each day, which nourishes you in some way, can help shift how you feel about work just a little, and can also be something that might lead to fresh avenues of opportunity. This might be a passion that you decide to devote some of your own time to, like a love for drawing that you channel into a ten-minute sketch every day, or maybe find an evening class you can learn from. You might also find opportunities within your current work day to do a project that you care about and that might help you transition to other areas.

This is starting to sound a lot like job crafting. I love this phrase, and when I learnt about it I felt like it suddenly made sense of what I'd been doing for a while. Job crafting is the idea that we can tweak and tailor our jobs to some extent, to make them more of a good fit for us. I can't radically change the content of what I do – if I'm employed to be a psychologist I can't suddenly say I want to write articles instead of providing therapy – but if I know I love creating things with words as well as doing my clinical work then I can seize opportunities to write patient information, or to be involved in therapeutic writing groups with people. Sometimes we can extend this into 'side hustles' or portfolio careers, where we spend time outside of work on the things we want to learn or nourish, or where we create a bespoke working week which involves a mix of jobs, so that we can get the balance that suits us.

Job crafting can involve actively changing what you do, how you do it and who you interact with. In a broad sense, it can also be about how you perceive your work. So, for example, an education administration job which might seem boring could be reframed as a way to help students and make sure that they are accessing the learning they are entitled to: suddenly it seems a lot more engaging and important.[2]

The idea of job crafting came from Jane Dutton and Amy Wrzesniewski.[3] They started to study it about twenty years ago, when they got interested in how people alter their jobs to make them more meaningful: hospital cleaners who change the way they think about their job to think of themselves as a key part in healing, and consultants who manage to negotiate incorporating teaching and learning as key parts of what they do because they enjoy it so much. Even in jobs which seem strictly set up there is often room to request to be in a specific department, for example in policing asking to be in a role which liaises more with victims of a particular sort of crime.

A good starting point for job crafting is often looking back at a couple of weeks of work and noticing when you felt happiest or in a state of 'flow' (fully absorbed in what you are doing). Those times are the sweet spot of a working day. Making sure you have a task nearly every day which you gel with can be one way of crafting your job into something you enjoy more.

Job crafting can be something that managers can encourage in their supervisees, often with the effect of improving job satisfaction. However, the way that a job gets crafted needs to fit in with the goals of the organization, or else it can end up making someone less productive instead of more. Or more productive in work they want to be productive in but to the detriment of what they are actually being paid to do. The ideal world is to work out a job plan where both the employee and the organization are happy.

Sometimes, even in a job where what we do is just what we like to do, and we are liaising with people we like and thinking about our work as something meaningful, we can still get caught up in worries that won't go away. For some people this can relate to perfectionism.

It's an old joke that if you're asked what your flaws are in a job interview you should say you are a perfectionist. But actually clinical perfectionism is a real problem. When I first heard about the term I thought it referred to clinicians who are perfectionists (and, to be fair, this is quite common), but in fact it means a level of perfectionism which is so great it gets in the way of your everyday life, causing distress and preventing you from doing what you want. Not everyone has clinical levels of perfectionism, but knowing about some of the treatments for this can aid those of us with lower levels of perfectionism which can still be less than helpful.

Perfectionism involves holding ourselves to unrelenting and exacting standards which are impossible to achieve.[4] It leads people to continue to work at something to try to get it absolutely perfect, rather than stopping when it is good enough, or accepting some flaws. It's a really hard thing to tackle, because commonly if we're motivated to make things perfect then any suggestion of trying less hard can seem like an invitation to be mediocre. In fact, trying even 20 per cent less hard, if we are being a perfectionist, often makes no noticeable difference to the outcome of what we are working on, but can make a massive difference to how much time and effort we are having to put in. There is a quote, often attributed to Voltaire, which says that 'perfect is the enemy of the good'. This idea, that striving for perfection can stop us being able to settle for something which is perfectly good enough, can be a helpful one to bear in mind.

Perfectionism can be exhausting, because the relentless standards that perfectionists deal with are internal – they never go away. Unfortunately, I think our exam system in the UK encourages this sort of thinking, and I've seen several young people for treatment whose unrelenting standards around exam results have caused them huge anxiety. If these same standards continue into adulthood they can cause real problems at work, and at home.

Think about Amy. She has spent the last six years training to be a doctor and she is about to become a GP. She doesn't feel happy about this, she feels exhausted. Her high standards mean she checks and double-checks her work to make sure it's correct. It means she has always worked later on placement than any of her colleagues and she continues to think about work outside of hours, worrying over decisions she has made and notes she has written. Was she comprehensive enough in explaining her actions? Were her choices 100 per cent correct? The trouble is that in medicine, as in many difficult professions, there isn't always one correct answer, and there is always more work to be done. Amy never feels that she has finished her shift.

Amy doesn't want to continue for the rest of her career like this, working all the hours there are and always feeling like she is somehow failing. At the same time, any thought of being less exacting makes her feel that she would be compromising patient safety and doing a rubbish job.

Treatment for clinical perfectionism involves several parts.[5] The first step is to think about making a change, and what the pros and cons are of this. It's really hard to let go of perfectionist behaviours, without feeling like everything is going to go to pot. However, thinking about the costs of perfectionism can prompt people to be up for considering trying a change. It's just not sustainable to continually be putting in 100 per cent, which can lead to exhaustion and burnout. It's also not helpful to constantly be having a go at yourself for not being perfect.

Once there is the possibility of making a shift, the next step is thinking together about trying some experiments in action. Amy should think about how often she checks her notes, and whether there might be room for checking them less. So, continue writing good notes but try a week of reading through them only once and seeing whether anything is different. To try this is excruciatingly hard at first, but Amy notices that she doesn't make any more mistakes than before. She goes one step further, and experiments with writing bullet-point notes rather than long paragraphs of prose, something she's seen colleagues doing. It saves her time and she gets surprising feedback that it is clearer for her colleagues to read than the longer, more involved version.

Thinking about the thoughts we experience in perfectionism is also important. Like any thoughts, it's easy to fall into traps of thinking in unhelpful ways. Black and white thinking, where everything is either awful or brilliant, is one example. For Amy, she feels like if she isn't perfect as a doctor then she would be dangerous and incompetent. She doesn't think this about any of her colleagues, but when she thinks about herself, she has hugely exacting standards. This goes along with some unhelpful rules she has for herself: things like 'I must do things perfectly, or I will be an incompetent doctor', 'If I don't check my work, I will make a serious mistake' and 'If I don't try harder than everyone else, I will fail.' Some of these rules had their roots in previous experiences, but when Amy is able to unpick these even the previous experiences can be seen in a different light. Amy remembers having failed a test when she hadn't worked as hard as usual. When she looked back, though, she had still got a good mark, just not as high as she was used to. She also remembers stories from medical school of clinical errors. She has not made one herself, but the thought of it fills her with dread. When she thought of errors her friends had made, she was able to see that none of them had been life-threatening, and that making a mistake sometimes is human, and can even lead to further learning and better practice.

Over time, Amy develops new rules for herself: 'I must try hard and check my work once but checking more than this is unhelpful', 'I must make sure my care is good enough, but I can't always be perfect, I am human' and 'I can try 20 per cent less hard and things will still be good enough.' Amy's feedback from colleagues and patients improves as she becomes less fixed on checking everything and staying late. She feels more rested and more able to listen to what people are telling her. She makes space in her week for herself, as well as her work, and uses mindfulness practices whenever she has a few minutes, like in the car before she gets out to go into work, or on the bus if she is taking public transport. She feels more confident that she will be able to manage the pressures of being a GP. The way Amy speaks to herself also slightly shifts, from having a go at herself to being kinder and gentler, like the self-talk we thought about in April. Amy tries to remember that total perfection is impossible, and that 'good enough' is enough.

Perfectionism can be a huge source of stress at work, and one that often largely comes from within ourselves, with unrelenting standards which we find it hard to drop. Sometimes the causes of stress are not so much about how we approach something, though, but about the conditions of the workplace. Someone else's unrelenting standards, for example, or expectations which are just impossible to meet. Working in mental health wards was a job I loved, but it did come with stresses. The work was never really finished – there was always something more that could be done. And worries about whether people were going to be OK was something which I found hard to leave at the door when I went home. Every job has something like this, though: something which can stay with you outside of hours and make it hard to 'switch off'. This is often the flip side of doing a job you care about – you're probably more likely to care about it all the time, not just in work hours.

Even in jobs which are inherently stressful, there are ways of managing work stress which can be helpful. One of these is being aware of how we respond to stress. Each of us does this in a slightly different way, a way that is unique. When I teach groups of NHS staff about this, I refer to it as a stress signature. Our stress signature involves our bodies, and also our thoughts and behaviours. For example, when I start to get stressed at work, my body has some warning signs for me. Tense shoulders, tense jaw and tension head-aches are all nudges that prompt me to think about what I'm doing and try to take a break, stretch, and look at my diary to see if I can cancel a meeting or two. Similarly, if I notice that I am starting to think in either a very ruminative way, going over things I've done and having a go at myself for not doing them well enough, or if I start catastrophizing about how terrible things are going to be in the future, then this might be a sign that I need a rest. And behavioural cues that might show up for me include being snappier than usual, or very reactive to emails.

These behavioural and bodily signs are different for everyone, and in some ways it doesn't matter what the signs are. What matters is that we know what they are so that we can spot them and realize when our stress levels are starting to creep up. It's much easier to do something about it when our stress levels are just starting to increase rather than when they are feeling sky high.

Another way of thinking about stress which I love for its simplicity is the stress bucket. Put simply, we all have a stress bucket that we carry around with us. Some days it is fuller than others. And some days we are more able than others to manage the stress. Imagine a bucket being filled up with water from lots of different sources: these are the different stresses that might bother us daily. Some will be work stress: our to-do list, a colleague we are not seeing eye to eye with, a presentation we feel nervous about... Others will be issues from our home life: a row with a loved one, a money worry, a sleepless night. The more stress we have going in, the fuller the bucket will be, until it might overflow, and we feel unable to cope.

We all also have holes that we can punch in the bottom of the bucket which allow the stress to dissipate. The holes might be an exercise class to blow off steam, a chat with a good friend, asking for more support from a manager... Some of those holes might not be so helpful, though. They might accidentally funnel stress back in. Drinking to help ourselves relax but having a glass too many and feeling hungover and vulnerable, staying up late watching our favourite programme and then feeling exhausted and emotional the next day, enjoying some delicious chocolate but then overdoing it and feeling unhealthy, using retail therapy and then racking up debt on a credit card... we've all got some coping strategies which are unhelpful. At the pointy end are even more self-sabotaging behaviours like self-harm and alcoholism, but it's really all just a matter of degree. It's human to use some coping styles that work in the short term but not in the medium to long term (as we'll think about again in December).

In that list of things which punch holes in my bucket, I include mindfulness, and this is also one of the practices which research has shown is helpful in reducing work-related stress.[6] I'd like to drop in a caveat here, though, because mindfulness isn't for everyone. If you've tried it and hate it, or feel that it makes you feel more stressed, I think it's absolutely fine to skip this bit. However, if you haven't ever tried it and you just don't like the sound of it because it's got a bit too popular, try to stick with this and give it a chance. Because research really does suggest it can be useful.

We met mindfulness in August when we thought about managing anger. Mindfulness is the practice of being in the here and now, instead of worrying about what hasn't happened yet (and might not), or ruminating over things that have already happened (and we can't change). It sounds so deliciously simple, but that doesn't mean it's easy to do.

The word 'practice' really is key here. If we sit down out of the blue and expect to be able to meditate for an hour without any build-up, we will definitely be disappointed. Our minds jump around, from one thing to another – that's just what they do. Mindfulness doesn't necessarily stop this, but doing a little bit often makes it more possible to feel slightly detached from all that jumping around, and to watch the thoughts come and go. Mindfulness doesn't still our mind or make us never have thoughts that cause us pain, but with regular practice we are often more able to be in the here and now and also reap a whole host of benefits for our physical and mental health.[7] Now, again, there are actually some people who find that mindfulness practices make them more stressed, but the majority of people really benefit from having a go. There are so many apps and YouTube videos out there that it's easy to try short practices for a week or two and see for yourself if it makes a difference. I definitely notice when I've had a run of doing mindfulness practice: I feel less reactive, and a greater sense of peace and happiness, even in the midst of tricky situations.

Another thing which often punches holes in people's stress buckets to let stress out is talking about the problem. As we learnt in the red-hot anger month of August, the way we discuss difficulties can affect how we feel. Venting about angry feelings, as we thought about then, can just make us feel angrier, and annoy people around us too. There's something that's worth being aware of in relation to traumatic material here as well. Some people, such as mental and physical health professionals, work in jobs where they are hearing about traumas that other people have experienced; the same applies to the police, who deal with information about assaults, and anyone involved in child protection, including teachers, nursery workers and social workers. In these professions, it can sometimes be tempting to offload on work colleagues about difficult things that you have heard. The research on this suggests that this is not very helpful, however, and can result in lots of people knowing information that they don't necessarily need to, and whole teams becoming traumatized.

Instead, a framework called low-impact disclosure suggests that before sharing something traumatic, you first check someone has time to speak, then ask permission to share, and then only share the minimum information to begin with and see if that is enough.[8] This prevents scenarios of people ambushing you by the kettle at work and launching into a long traumatic story when you only have two minutes and you're just trying to get your own head together. Suggesting this strategy to colleagues for how best to deal with information which we find traumatic is sometimes a controversial idea, because people can worry that it will prevent others from talking, but it can be a great springboard for group discussion, encouraging whole teams to think together about how to share difficult information. Apart from anything else, this also minimizes the amount of personal information about other people which is shared, which is a good thing, but it also tends to help teams feel better. That's not to say that if you're dealing with something stressful, heavy or traumatic at work, it's not good to seek out one-to-one support to process it, just that making sure you are careful about how and where you do that can reap dividends.

Thinking about how to deal with stress at work is important, but so is the flip side – thinking about how to celebrate the good stuff. We often forget this, but it can keep us going when times get tough. In the helping professions there is a term – compassion fatigue – which describes the feeling of running out of the ability to care as much as before. There's also an alternative term – compassion satisfaction – which is the enjoyment we get from caring for and helping others. Celebrating those moments when we have made a difference in our work, whether it is in a caring profession or in something totally different, can boost our sense of purpose and our sense of efficacy. Yet how often do we do this, either on an individual or a team level? When teams learn from previous experiences it tends to be learning from mistakes. When we think back over our performance at work it is often to reflect on how we can do better. Yet we can also purposefully take the time to print out emails where people have thanked us, to look over cards from people who have acknowledged something meaningful we have done for them and to notice moments in our day where we've had a really nice time, or at least felt like we've done our job well. Even a small amount of this can make a really big difference.

Sometimes, no matter how much energy we put into crafting our job and appreciating the good stuff in it, we might find that it's time to make a change. It could be that we've outgrown the role and it doesn't feel as good a fit as before. It could be that the culture feels toxic and is getting us down. It could be that we love it but we want to stretch ourselves in some new way. This isn't to say that we can't learn and grow from staying still: staying in one place can also give us new opportunities and deeper connections, and that too can be deeply fulfilling.

If we're feeling work stress, though, and if the things we've tried on an individual level to manage it haven't helped, then it's worth knowing that research shows that the main interventions that reduce staff stress are those that tackle both what we can do as individuals working in a tricky situation and what the organization is doing to improve conditions. If the organization isn't changing, and the job is really stressful, or you feel the culture is toxic or the working practices are bad, then there may be a limit to how much you can reduce your stress. In this situation you might be faced with thinking about how to leave. And this in itself brings up managing change (see January) and loss (see October). It also brings up endings.

Endings are something that therapists really like to think about. There is plenty written on how to end a therapeutic relationship in the best way, to make sure that the client feels supported even after sessions have finished, and that they have a chance to say what they need to say to the therapist before they stop. Different models of therapy do things differently here, as ever, but I think all therapists agree that it's important to end well. All endings are a loss, and as such they might resonate with other losses that a client has experienced, and take on even more significance than they might otherwise. This can be true even when they are endings that are anticipated well in advance or wished for: a promotion which means leaving a familiar role, a child leaving home to go on to take the next steps in their life, or the conclusion of a course of therapy because things feel more resolved or possible.

In therapy, it's key to make sure that the ending isn't abrupt. You wouldn't typically discuss ending out of the blue in a session and then never see each other again. In some models of therapy you'd know from the start roughly how many sessions to expect, and in other, more open-ended types of therapy you would discuss the likelihood of ending quite a way in advance. This gives you both the chance to think about how the ending feels, what it means, what coping strategies will be taken forward from therapy, and any resonances with other endings in the person's life. It's not always a loss that might be resonant, it could be a celebration: graduation is a type of ending too, and one that we typically feel good about.

Ending a job can carry these different possibilities as well. We might feel a mix of feelings even about a place from where we feel ready to leave. We might usefully think about what we want to take with us, and I don't mean the stapler or the mug we used. Which memories will we treasure? Which contacts will we maintain? What do we want to celebrate that we have done? What are we grateful for from our colleagues and friends?

Some jobs are easier to leave than others, and if you're leaving a job which you feel is painful or toxic in some way it can be hard to know how to handle it. Leaving a job because you feel that the workplace culture is too slow to change, or damaging in some way, it can be hard to know how much to feed this back. Sometimes there are opportunities to do this: well-managed exit interviews or thoughtful questionnaires, but often in a workplace which is not functioning healthily these things are absent and it can feel unsafe to talk about the parts that aren't working, or can be hard to identify who you can speak to about the culture or structure of the place. If it doesn't feel possible to give your point of view on the things that haven't been good, then trying to leave with as little negative impact and as much positive impact as possible can be a helpful focus: making handovers easier for the next person, rounding things up as much as you can and thinking about what you have achieved in the time there. It's hard in the cut and thrust of leaving, but making a bit of space to write down the answers to some of those questions in the preceding paragraph can really help to feel like you are moving on intentionally.

Whether we stay or go, whether we stick or twist, it is always us inhabiting the different roles that we are in. We bring our personal selves to our professional roles, and our personal and professional lives affect each other. Reflecting on some of the overlaps – the way we are with other people at work, the patterns we bring with our expectations of ourselves and others – it's worth investing the time to think through what goes well and what you would do differently, because one thing is for sure, you'll get the chance again. We might have left school, but we haven't left the chance to learn behind. Life has a clever way of presenting us again and again with similar challenges in different situations and allowing us to try different ways of managing them. Looking back and feeling like we've learnt, and grown and changed, at least a little, can only be a good thing, however painful that learning might sometimes be at the time.

MAKING THE MOST OF WORK

Key Ideas

1. If work is stressing you out, find out what's in your control and what's not. It can help you to decide where to target your energy for most chance of change.

2. Consider job crafting. How can you tweak your day-to-day work reality to make it incorporate a little bit of what you fancy? What are the favourite parts of your week? How can you grow that aspect of your role? If changes aren't possible in work, what passion project can you devote some energy to in your own time?

3. Don't let the quest for perfection be the enemy of the good enough. Are there perfectionist tendencies which are getting in your way of enjoying your achievements at work? If so, experiment with dropping some of these and see what happens – you might be surprised.

4. Visualize or draw out your own stress bucket and see what is causing stress and how to puncture it. How can you increase stress-busting behaviours? Are there any stress releases which are inadvertently hindering you? Try to cut back on those and see how it makes a difference.

5. Mindfulness isn't for everyone, but if you haven't tried it, give it a go, for just a few minutes in your daily routine for a couple of weeks, and see if it has any effect. I'd recommend looking up Mark Williams' three-minute breathing space (available on Spotify), Headspace (free videos on YouTube and an app with a free trial) and the book *Mindfulness: Finding Peace in a Frantic World* by Mark Williams and Danny Penman.[9] Alternatively, if you want a send-up of mindfulness, *The Ladybird Book of Mindfulness* is quite funny.

6. If you're working in a stressful job where traumatic information is being shared, think how this is being done and whether it is necessary. Even if your job isn't that trauma-related you can still think about asking permission before leaping into a moan – it helps to stop a culture of venting.

7. What's the good stuff? There must be a reason you're staying where you are, so try to remember the good bits about what you're doing. What do you like? What do other people value about you? Keep a box of thank-you cards or positive emails so you can delve into it if you're having a difficult day.

8. If you do decide to move on from a job, think about how you manage the ending in a way that leaves you and the organization feeling as good as possible about it. Endings can be losses but they can also be graduations to celebrate or chances for a moment of reflection. There is more about coping with loss in the next chapter too.

9. If you think perfectionism is becoming a real problem in your life, then the book *Overcoming Perfectionism*, by Roz Shafran, Sarah Egan and Tracey Wade, might be helpful.

10

OCTOBER

Falling Leaves

Coping with Loss

Octber in the UK is full of falling leaves being trodden into the pavement and piling up roads. The shapes of leaves in bright yellows, reds and oranges appear first like stencils on the ground and then turn into faint skeletons as footsteps and tyres erode them. Autumn into winter can feel like a painful transition. The cold makes us tense up and the nights drawing in can bring a feeling of claustrophobia, as we start and end our working days in the dark. Trees become bare as we lose the brightness and carefree feel of summer and the prettiness of autumn. We're left with a darker time.

The old Celtic festival of Samhain (pronounced sah-win) is on the first day of November, but is often celebrated on the last day of October (now replaced by Halloween). Marking the halfway point between autumn equinox and winter solstice, the festival was associated with going deeper into the darker part of the year. Harvests were taken in and trees shed their leaves. It was supposedly a time when the boundary between this world and the 'otherworld' grew thinner; spirits could visit, and souls of the dead could return to their homes. Places were set at the table for lost loved ones, much in the way that in Mexico, at a similar time of year, the Day of the Dead festival is a celebration of friends and family members who have died. In Mexico elaborate altars are created and graves are decorated with candles, flowers and gifts for the dead. At this shift of seasons, the natural cycles of the plants and trees around us seem amplified. In reality, things are changing all the time, all year round, but this time of year, like other changes of the seasons, can feel like a noticeable still frame of transition.

Autumn and winter happen every year, but the change can still feel melancholy. It makes me think of other cycles of loss we experience throughout our lives. We will all be touched by loss in one way or another, whether that's the ending of a relationship, the loss of people we love through bereavement, or other losses which might be couched as more 'minor', but which can loom just as large. In this chapter we think about what can help us to cope with losses, why we can sometimes be extra-sensitive to loss, and how we can hold ourselves kindly in the face of it all.

Grief is suffering or distress over loss. Loss doesn't have to mean a bereavement but that is one loss that we will all experience throughout our lives, as people we love die. We're really bad, in the UK at least, at talking about death. It's going to happen to us all, but we spend very little time acknowledging that, even when it is obviously quite close. It's painful to think about it, this ultimate separation, so we try not to.

There are a handful of exceptions: initiatives like death cafés, whose facilitators try to encourage conversations about death, dying and bereavement; the Good Grief Trust, which has a wealth of information on its website;[1] death doulas, practitioners who help individuals and families to have a 'good' death; and staff who work in hospices, managing both the physical and emotional pain associated with the end of life. On the whole, though, people tend to feel awkward about how to talk about death. Almost as if talking about it will either tempt fate or make grief worse somehow.

Our reluctance to talk about death extends, I think, to our awkwardness in the face of other losses. Grief doesn't only relate to death: relationship break-ups, redundancies, traumatic experiences of all kinds, are hard for us to negotiate. People often feel like they don't know what to say, and so they avoid saying anything, or make a joke, or make a swift 'everything is fine' type of remark, to try to tidy up the messiness of raw emotion which comes along with grief.

If there is anything which is in the public consciousness about grief, it's the idea that it moves through stages. This comes from the writing of Elisabeth Kübler-Ross, author of *On Death and Dying*[2] and *On Grief and Grieving*.[3] She wrote about five stages: denial, anger, bargaining, depression and acceptance. She never intended these to be seen as a linear progression, but somehow they have often been taken to be a process that we should all go through, to get to the end point of acceptance. Elisabeth Kübler-Ross actually suggested we might go back and forth through any of these stages, flipping back to denial at any point, or fast-forwarding to depression. The theory is just that as well: one theoretical way of thinking about some of the emotions that are present, not a sure-fire catalogue of what we're bound to experience. Some people experience other emotions: horror, for example, or relief, or emotional numbness. Kübler-Ross's writing is helpful as a jumping-off point for conversations about loss and the many different feelings that accompany it, but less helpful if we see it as a roadmap for what is going to happen. It's extra tricky if on top of dealing with grief we are also somehow thinking that we're doing it wrong because our grief isn't following a path that we think it should do.

One thing Elisabeth Kübler-Ross's model does which is useful is to encourage us to see grief as a process, and as a process which involves multiple different emotions. Grief can sound like it should just be one thing, but whenever I have felt it, I have experienced it more as many different feelings and thoughts. These have included anger at people who have died, or at situations which have happened not as I wanted them to; deep sadness, which often takes me by surprise; and a kind of wishful thinking: running through how things might've been in a parallel universe, if the person I am grieving were still alive, or if the situation I feel grief about had happened otherwise. The different griefs I have felt in response to different losses have also been affected by the process of the loss: the sudden, unexpected death of a younger person felt absolutely horrific to me; while the expected death of an older person, with whom I had had the time and opportunity to be with and speak to in the run-up, felt hugely sad but less violent.

These feelings and thoughts take emotional energy, and grief can be exhausting and feel all-consuming, whether it relates to a death or to another type of loss. It can make us forget things, misplace things and have trouble functioning in the world as we normally would. In the aftermath of one relationship break-up back in London I did all manner of absent-minded things, including misplacing my passport (later finding it down the back of a bookcase) and leaving the keys to my flat at work (meaning I had to let myself into a dark, deserted office to try to find them, at half eleven at night after I'd been to the pub). Grief can also sometimes feel like anxiety, like nothing is safe. It can cause panic attacks as we flail around trying to carry on as before when there has been a seismic shift in our reality. It can have other physical symptoms too, which feel as real as any other physical illness, including headaches and bodily aches and pains.

Just as we can avoid talking to others about their losses and their griefs, so we can avoid a conversation with ourselves about this as well. Avoiding thinking about loss is one way of dealing with it (the denial from Kübler-Ross's approach). Saying that we're 'fine' after a break-up, determinedly going out on the town to prove it, is one example of this. Snapping that we just don't want to talk about it is another.

We can't run from this stuff forever, though, and while it's not necessarily helpful to stew in feelings of sadness, there is something, sometimes, in allowing ourselves to feel grief to process the loss. Psychodynamic theory talks about the 'manic defence', of keeping so busy that we can't feel difficult emotions. CBT would talk more about avoidance, but it might just be a different name for a similar process. Sometimes we need to reflect on the difficult and the painful to make some meaning of it. Not that there is always a trite reframing to be done, but some making sense of it all, even if the sense that we end up arriving at is 'this is really painful'.

With painful break-ups or lost opportunities there often is at least a glimmer of a sense that things might be better down the line, that these things work out for the best somehow, whereas with losses such as death of a loved one there is much less comfort available. If we're lucky then the sense of a good death might be there: a lack of pain, a chance to say everything we wanted to say and to hear everything our loved one wanted to tell us. In more sudden deaths, especially of younger people, there is little comfort. Either way, no matter how a loss has occurred, the mental reconfiguration of the world that is necessary, to realize that that person is no longer here with us, is huge, and the new reality feels harsh.

We don't only grieve for people who have died, or for relationships that have ended. We can grieve for ourselves too: for lost parts of ourselves, for experiences we had which we wish we hadn't, or conversely for the things we wished had happened for us but haven't. We can mourn the roads not taken, the opportunities not granted, and just the messy old way that things unfold sometimes. The poem 'The Road Not Taken', by Robert Frost, captures this sense of loss of an unknown future, the same loss we thought about in January's chapter on decision-making.

In the therapy room, grief is sometimes part of the bigger picture of what people are bringing. Usually grief, over time, doesn't go away but becomes more manageable. Sometimes it doesn't, though, and traumatic grief is when someone has a post-traumatic reaction to a death or a loss. Post-traumatic reactions relate to how our brains process the experience we have had, or rather how much our brains might struggle to process it. The diagnosis of a post-traumatic reaction isn't made in the first month after a traumatic experience, as it's normal for us to take some time to process what has happened and to feel preoccupied with it. In fact, treatments aren't offered in this period because it's better to 'watch and wait' to see if trauma responses settle down.

Post-trauma reactions can be brutal. Imagine something terrible happening, and then being forced to replay that thing on a loop in your thoughts when you're least wanting to. This could be in the form of flashbacks, where it literally feels like you are back in whichever traumatic event you have experienced, so it is happening now; or it could be in the form of intrusive thoughts, memories, or nightmares, occurring unbidden. Much as you try to avoid thinking about, talking about or remembering the event, it keeps turning up in your head. In fact the trying not to think about it can make things worse. You might not even realize it, but all this makes you feel in a permanent state of high alert. This might feel like being permanently jumpy or on edge. It might show up as irritation, pushing your loved ones away from you. Or it might show up as fearfulness of other things going wrong, or the same thing happening again. You might break into a sweat, or experience panic attacks where it feels like you can't breathe. You might feel a sense of guilt or shame or self-blame around whatever occurred, a sense that it was somehow your fault.

These are all common trauma reactions, and they can happen to anyone, to a greater or lesser degree, with milder reactions still having the potential to be preoccupying and warrant attention. Trauma reactions tend to occur when there has been a fear of something bad happening, like death or the possibility of death, either your own or someone else's. It doesn't matter whether or not this happened, and you can still have a trauma reaction even if other people don't think the event was that bad (such as in a near-miss car crash).

This way of overcoming trauma memories might seem counter-intuitive, but one approach (from CBT) involves going through them in more detail, often with someone else. The reason our brain presents us with the trauma memories that we want to avoid is because they haven't been processed properly in our memory. A common analogy used in therapy is to describe this like having a messy wardrobe. If your wardrobe is so stuffed full of scrunched-up clothes that every time you open the door they all fall out on you, or the jumper sleeves get stuck in the door and keep opening it, then the way to sort it is to take them all out and fold them up more neatly so they stay where you've put them.

With memories, because traumatic events tend to activate the primitive parts of our brains, which are more to do with emotion (especially fear), this can interfere with the usual memory encoding which goes on. To store these memories better we need to be able to consider them with a less fear-based part of our brain. The rumination and intrusive thoughts that post-trauma reactions bring with them is our brain's attempt to tidy the memories away to some degree, but because they are 'hot' with emotion, it's hard to do. Part of what trauma therapy can do is to help people take the heat out of the memory, by helping the person remember that they are in the here and now, that they are safe, and often enabling them to introduce new, kinder thoughts about their own role in what happened, and more stable thoughts about what the event might mean.

Traumatic grief reactions can involve intrusive memories about events leading up to a death, or the death itself, or events after a death.[4] They might also involve grief around an experience: for example a near-death experience, belief that someone was in grave danger or an experience which happened in a traumatic way that was far from what was hoped for. Clinical-level post-traumatic stress disorder, which gets in the way of someone being able to live their life as they would like, is best dealt with by an evidence-based talking therapy[5] rather than any kind of attempt at self-help, but some of the same principles from post-trauma work can be useful even if there isn't a full-blown traumatic reaction. These include things like piecing together a timeline of what happened, or writing about it or making drawings, to enable the brain to process it and 'tidy it away'.

Being able to remind ourselves that we are in the here and now and that right now we are safe is one important ingredient. Being able to make sense of difficult things that have happened is another, and often useful in being able to move on from them. This doesn't mean creating a Pollyanna narrative of 'thank goodness it all worked out in the end' or 'things always happen for a reason'. Sometimes a horrible experience is just a horrible experience. But being able to have a clear sense of what has happened, when, why (if that is a possibility), and what our role was in it, can be useful to help lay something to bed. The way we do this doesn't have to involve talking to someone else. It might involve writing, art-making, or just thinking about what happened, as long as we don't get stuck in a rumination loop.

Writing about lost loved ones brings another dimension, as often it can feel like a way to keep their memory alive. Talking about them too, and celebrating who they were, including all their facets, even the trickier bits, can also help. I remember in my early twenties going into work after my grandfather had died, and my supervisor at the time (a clinical psychologist) asking me what he was like. What a great question! And one which is hardly ever asked. The chance to talk about him felt like holding him near in a way which a 'sorry for your loss' just wouldn't have created. The best funerals manage to do this too, to conjure up a sense of the real person.

I wonder about other losses as well, whether it might be helpful to be allowed to really explore and make sense of them. What was it that we had wished for and which we need to then let go of? What other reality would we be living had things worked out differently? How did things happen the way that they did? And where would we be if they had not? What sort of person would we be, with what alternative reality?

The further on through life we go, the more choices we have made and the fewer options it can seem that we have. There's nothing wrong with sometimes lamenting those other realities, those other selves that we might have been. Sometimes by describing them we might see small glimmers of possibilities that we could revisit: a hobby we want to take up, a different value we want to pay attention to, a playfulness we want to resurrect somehow. It's easy to feel that as our creative constraints get greater as we go through life there is no room for manoeuvre, but in fact there is always some wiggle room, and sometimes room for huge seismic movements! If we never acknowledge the losses or griefs we might feel then it's hard to be alert to the possibilities we might want to explore.

One thing I am alert to when listening to people who come to see me for psychology sessions is when they experience a reaction to a loss which they feel is disproportionate. If they say, 'It feels bigger than it should', this might mean that they are giving themselves a hard time for feeling a totally proportionate reaction to a difficult loss, or it might be something else.

When we have big losses in our lives which we haven't had the chance to process, they can sometimes come back and surprise us. Memories might get triggered by a smaller loss, leaving us feeling totally at sea without knowing why our reaction is so huge. What we're experiencing is a kind of emotional resonance with what has gone before, the other loss which we felt keenly and haven't fully mourned. Sometimes these losses go right back to early relationships we had with people we were attached to: our early caregivers, for instance (which we thought about a bit in June, with attachment theory). Other times the losses might be fresher: for example, a painful break-up that we never quite understood. Whenever the grief of a loss reappears it's often worth spending a bit of time with the loss that is resurfacing, and using talking to others, or writing, or creative endeavours, to try to approach it in a helpful way. For really overwhelming grief which persists I think it's helpful to seek assistance from a trained therapist, because it can be very hard to do this by ourselves.

Just as we considered, in September, endings at work, any ending can have some resonance with a loss. Let's think about Tara. She has just broken up with a partner who she has had a tricky relationship with. The break-up was a fairly mutual decision: she and her ex found themselves on a repeating loop by having the same row and couldn't find a way to move past the obstacles it threw up. They wanted different things for the relationship: she wanted to feel a sense of progress, but planning for the future made him feel stifled and claustrophobic. In the mix was a tendency for him to speak to her in a way that undermined how she felt about herself. He was careless about how he criticized her and it very quickly wore her down.

There were good reasons for the break-up and, rationally, Tara thought they had made the right decision, but... she just felt awful. She found herself thinking about her ex all the time, crying unexpectedly, and feeling totally bereft. Her friends thought she should join a dating app and get over the relationship, but the suggestion made her feel sick and weepy. She felt stuck.

Tara found herself thinking about other relationships which had ended too, and experiencing a sense of abandonment, aloneness and finality that she remembered from other times in her life, including a bereavement she had experienced as a teenager. She found that it was hard to get a satisfying response when she spoke to her friends and family about the break-up. She was so sensitive to what people said that she could easily feel tumbled down a rabbit hole of ruminating over what she could have done differently, or wishful thinking about how things might have been.

Tara used therapy sessions to talk about her ex and their relationship. As she did this, and used a journal to write things down, she realized there were repeating themes of positives and negatives. It was easier to think of the positives now they weren't together, but there had been negative things too: reasons for the break-up. In some ways Tara was mourning a relationship that she wished she had had, rather than the one which had ended.

In time Tara found that a balance of things helped. She didn't want to go out on the town yet, but hanging out with friends and asking them about their lives instead of spending all the time talking about her ex helped her to see things from a slightly different point of view. The world was still turning, things were still happening in that world, and she was still part of it.

Tara was also encouraged by therapy to think about how she would care for a good friend who was going through the same situation. She tried to encourage herself to eat healthily, do some gentle exercise and provide herself with opportunities to relax. Long baths with a podcast on so she couldn't go round and round in her own head, walks in the countryside with friends, time on her own too, and allowing herself to be upset, but not getting sucked into only thinking over and over what had already happened.

It was a balance of time spent mourning and time spent trying to keep on keeping on that helped get Tara through, until one day she felt like things were not quite as bad. Someone asked her if she was single at a party and she didn't feel terrible answering. The same stuff had still gone on, but she was more able to feel a slight distance from it. As time went on Tara went up and down with this feeling. Some days the loss felt really close again, sitting on her shoulder, and other days she could see it from a way away. As months passed, she spoke about herself more and more in therapy, and the space the ended relationship took up got smaller.

Tara hasn't forgotten the loss; it's just become folded into the rest of her life in a more manageable way. It is, however, possible to forget even the hugest loss, momentarily. I remember periods of grieving, both for my grandparents and for the end of a relationship, where for the first few moments after waking I just hadn't registered yet that those losses had happened. There was this lovely, brief, moment of pause, before I remembered and felt sad again.

Even years after their deaths I find myself wanting to introduce my grandparents to someone or tell them about something. In some respects this is a way of carrying them with me. It's comforting. When they died, I felt like they had left the party early, and I wished I'd had longer to speak to them. I've tried instead to hold on to the times we did have together, and think about the things I'd tell them if they were still here. Still talking to people who have died isn't mad, it's comforting. The traditions of Samhain and Day of the Dead realize this, and help us to celebrate the connection we have to others who are long gone, instead of trying to squash it and pretend it's not there.

Grief is in some ways the flip side of the coin from love. We suffer because we have cared deeply about someone or something. A risk, when grief is overwhelming, is that we shut down and refuse to be open to caring that much again, because the loss is so great that the idea of having such hurt again feels insurmountable.

To get through the smaller daily losses and disappointments of life, and the bigger sadnesses which totally floor us, is not about being graceful in the face of grief. We don't have to do it neatly. It's about getting through it and surviving in a wild and tender time. The effects of grief can rumble on throughout our lives, which doesn't mean we will feel the same distress all the time, but which might mean that anniversaries or unexpected reminders of a person or an experience might take us back to it with a rush. If we've been gentle with ourselves and allowed ourselves to feel some of the emotions and think about some of the meaning around the loss, then these reminders will be less likely to blindside us. The sadness is still there but it's somehow more manageable and less immediate.

I don't believe in trying to find a bright side for every experience, or a lesson within it. Perhaps there is some use in finding the love in the loss, though. What is the thing or the person that we cared about? How can we honour that? In the tradition of Samhain, who would we want to invite to dine with us again? And how can we invite back the people who have gone, bringing them into our day-to-day life, to carry them with us? Is there a shared value we can cherish to honour them? Or a more everyday practice of thinking of them and what we would say to them if they were here? Or if our grief is for the loss of an experience, is there a new or past experience that we can try to hold dear? Not as compensation, but as a reminder of the things which did go as we had hoped, or which went even better than we'd imagined.

COPING WITH LOSS

Key Ideas

1. Loss is hard to talk about, but it's sometimes good to try to; or if talking is too hard, then try using writing, drawing, whatever helps you to process what has happened.

2. Loss provokes lots of different feelings, and there is no right way to experience these.

3. We don't have to be graceful in the face of loss; sometimes it's enough just to get through.

4. Finding balance can be key: a mix of time where it's possible to mourn and time where we reconnect with others to get a different perspective.

5. Thinking of how we would look after a good friend can help here too: tenderly ministering to our own selves in the way we would to someone else who is grieving.

6. With time, we might be able to think about how to honour the memory of our loss in a way that holds space for it without sucking us into a whirlpool of sadness. Sometimes honouring losses can even be joyful.

7. If the description of post-traumatic stress disorder was resonant for you, I recommend *Trauma is Really Strange*, by Steve Haines, for more on this subject. It's definitely worth speaking to your GP about access to talking therapies too.[6]

8. Another great resource on loss is Michael Rosen's *Sad Book*. It's written for children but it's a lovely read for adults as well.

11

NOVEMBER

The Joy of Missing Out

Valuing Rest

People come to therapy for all sorts of reasons. It might be because of a formal diagnosis of a mental health problem, or it might be a feeling that things could be better, a sneaky suspicion that there are some self-defeating patterns at work which are preventing something... happiness, fulfilment, success of some kind.

There is still stigma attached to coming for therapy. It's something people talk about more these days, but with care. It's fair enough to be careful about it – it's so personal that that's probably wise – but I don't think we're at the stage where therapy sessions are viewed in the same way as a GP appointment, for example.

Many of the people I have seen for therapy cover up how they are feeling underneath. Their friends, colleagues, family, don't necessarily know that they feel like they are struggling, or if they do they often don't realize the extent. They might seem successful, happy, able to get along, in some cases doing brilliantly in their studies or jobs. Sometimes the things that can help people to do all this stuff can be part of what keeps them feeling like life is tough, though. One of these things can be a relentless desire to push on regardless, and to ignore the warning signs that maybe it's time for a rest.

I recognize this in myself, although I'm getting better at slowing down when needed. I used to find it really hard to rest, and would end up planning multiple things and enjoying all of them a bit less because I was just so tired. I still have to rein myself in with it, but I remind myself of JOMO – the joy of missing out, instead of the fear of missing out. It's that feeling you get when instead of going out all you crave is to be able to stay in with a jacket potato and a box set. One of the nicest New Year's Eves I ever had was on my own in my flat, eating spaghetti and meatballs and writing. Sometimes staying in is the new going out.

November is a time of year when it's easy to feel tired. In the northern hemisphere, the clocks have fallen backwards now, ushering in the season of dark mornings and evenings. It can feel like we have spent the whole of our daylight hours at work. As we know from research into the effects of seasonal affective disorder,[1] less light can make us feel less happy and more fatigued. We can end up wanting to hibernate. That's not necessarily a bad thing. There's a lot to juggle in life, and we're probably all working hard in one way or another. How often are we properly making time to stop? For me, November feels like it should be less about pushing on through and more about lying down flat. At this time more than ever we really need to pay attention to rest.

And what happens to us if we don't? Let's think about Jack. He feels bad, but he's not sure why, and he wants it to stop. Jack is training as a psychiatrist and finding this rewarding but difficult. He has gone into a career in mental health because of some of his own experiences with family members, but he is increasingly feeling worried that he himself might be worn down by the work and unable to help people as much as he wants to. Jack has lots of things he does to help himself feel better. He goes out to the pub after work with his colleagues, he captains a football team one night a week and, every Saturday, he spends time online dating... he has a lot of stuff he DOES. On top of this he is working shifts, some of them night shifts.

Jack reliably finds that he cycles through feeling productive and on top of things, through to feeling overwhelmed and like there is too much on, then to feeling totally exhausted and getting a cold the minute he has a couple of days off. As soon as he has three days off in a row he gets ill. 'It's always when I stop,' he says, and thinks that maybe the answer is to just keep going.

Jack's experience is not uncommon. How often, when you have a break, do you find that you have a niggle of a sore throat or the start of a snotty cold? Have you noticed that it always seems to be when we stop that we get sick? It turns out there are good reasons why.

Our immune system is primitive. The same system that helps us fight off colds today is the one which evolved in a time when we would have been running away from sabre-toothed tigers. In prehistoric situations we needed to run fast, fight or play dead in order to survive. So the immune system evolved in a way which takes cues from our stress system. It postpones us getting sick if we are experiencing stress responses. It switches everything else off in order to be able to engage in fight or flight. This would have helped us with acute stresses like running away from a sabre-toothed tiger. The trouble is that our stresses nowadays go on for much longer. Our 'sabre-toothed tigers' are chronic stresses like work pressures, unhelpful relationships and financial worries.

When we are chronically stressed, our bodies are left flooded with stress hormones, such as cortisol, for a long time. Cortisol directly communicates with the immune system and regulates how it works. Most often this results in a lowering of immune surveillance when we are under stress. The immune system is downregulated, and can't be as vigilant or effective in combating the millions of things that we encounter daily. When the stress stops, the immune system can recover, and it then ramps up its response to all the bugs that were around but that it didn't fight. This is why we often end up sniffling just when we are about to have a deliciously anticipated holiday. We get sick after a period of stress has ended because the immune system can upregulate again and work to get rid of the infections we have picked up in this period.

If we do get sick, it is unhelpful to ignore our body's signals for needing rest. It's a sign our body's immune system is working, making us slow down. It might feel annoying, but resting sooner rather than later will help us to recover faster, and not listening to how our body feels is lining up trouble. Pushing through with a cold can end up exacerbating the illness until it feels like proper-nasty, wipes-you-out, feels-a-bit-scary, flu.

There are several important systems in our bodies. One of them, that we've already heard about above, is the 'threat system', the brain system involved in spotting a threat in the environment and preparing us to run, hide or fight. Back in the day this system helped us spot predators. Now it kicks in as we scan situations for social risks, work terrors, or relationship frights. The threat system overrides the immune system to make sure our energy is more concentrated on the current environment – postponing any immune response that may be needed now, until later.

A second system which is less talked about is the parasympathetic nervous system, involved in 'resting and digesting'. This system is also involved in attachments and closeness with others. It's one that kicks in when we are safe, secure and content. The soothing system. The 'rest and digest' system works in opposition to the 'fight or flight' system. When one is activated the other is downregulated, a bit like when we use a brake pedal or accelerator in a car. We wouldn't press both pedals at once. Similarly, the fight or flight system revs us up, and the rest and digest system calms us down. The two systems are both part of the autonomic nervous system (along with one other system, the enteric nervous system, which is more to do with the gut).

We don't just ping between feeling threatened or soothed – sometimes we're motivated to be chasing goals for good reasons, and a third system, our 'drive' system, kicks in, and gives us a sense of achievement when we succeed.[2]

Have a think... if you were dividing up your week by one of these systems, which category do most experiences fall into? Does your day-to-day tend to be threatening, soothing, or driven? Most people are not using the soothe system as much as the others. I certainly have to make a conscious effort to make sure I am doing things that are soothing, in amongst things that I am working hard at or feeling a bit nervous about. Connections in our brains get strengthened by use, so if we don't use a system as much it is also likely to be less easily triggered than the others. The more we feel threatened or revved up the easier it is to feel that way again.

Weirdly, because it doesn't sound very soothing, jumping in cold water also activates the parasympathetic system. This is one reason why cold-water swimming is supposed to be so beneficial for our mental health. It activates the vagus nerve, which is a long cranial nerve running from the brain to different organs and tissues in the body, responsible for regulating autonomic nervous system activity. Stimulating the vagal nerve through cold-water swimming (or even putting our face in a sink of cold water)[3] helps to slow our heart rate and relax our body. The practice of getting in a sauna and then throwing a bucket of cold water over yourself has solid foundations.

In the November of the year I moved to Bristol, I went on holiday, with the same man I had met on that internet date in May. We went to Iceland, flying from one dark and cold country to another even more dark and cold country. The daylight hours were limited and we spent a lot of time driving on the main ring road in the glooming darkness, trying to get from one monumental landscape to another before it got pitch-black. The people in Iceland seemed to know how to make the most of these limited hours of sunshine, though, and know how to appreciate the darkness too. Iceland's volcanic location means it has a huge array of geothermally heated pools, both naturally occurring ones and built swimming pools. We went swimming one day, in a public pool in Reykjavik, and they had a candle lit in reception, just as they did on the café tables in the local bakery. It made for a sense of cosiness and softness. Inside, in the indoor pool, we had it nearly to ourselves to swim lengths, only realizing afterwards that the reason it was so empty was that outside was where the real deal was. A series of saunas and increasingly hotter hot pools were full of people relaxing after their day at work, of course with the cold-water bucket there for in between hot sits and soaks. They knew how to rest.

Cold water aside, prioritizing the soothing system doesn't necessarily mean that we can't work intensively and then take a break. For some people this works well, as long as there is some recovery time at some point. Where things get extra-sticky is when stress isn't controllable. We can't decide when our work is going to give us a conflicting deadline, or when something emotionally hard is going to happen. If the stresses aren't avoidable and we can't change the level of demand that is upon us, then one thing we can do is build in time for nice things anyway. Even if huge stress is around, if there are some experiences of positive mood this can be protective. Finding small things that give us pleasure and peppering our lives with them as regularly as possible can make a big difference. There might be things we can fit into a working day: a coffee in a favourite mug, a few minutes to stand outside and breathe, a walk around the block at lunchtime, a two-minute stretch, a really nice sandwich. These reduce the contrast between our 'on' times and our rest. There might also be things we do at home: a daytime bath or shower at the weekend, a candle lit at breakfast, ten minutes of yoga before bed. These are little things, and they are usually possible even when it feels like we have no time (in fact they are even more necessary when it feels like we have no time).

As always, if there are elements of the stresses that are under our control then it's worth having a think about whether we're up for making changes. If the stress is that we're too busy, what can we put down? Would it help to allocate time in our diaries that is just for us to do nothing, and think of it like an appointment with ourselves? If it's something bigger like a job or a relationship causing stress, then taking steps to talk to trusted others about the dilemma and make small steps to changing things can help. Even in a very demanding job, making tweaks to things like how often you check your emails can reap rewards.

For Jack, when he looks at what he is doing day to day, he is mostly engaged in things which involve his drive system or his threat system. There is nothing there which involves the parasympathetic soothing system. Even lunch is eaten on the run. He struggles to think of things which he wants to do which are more restful. He hates baths, he dislikes meditation, he prefers things where he feels alive because he is moving fast or dealing with problems of some kind. Eventually he settles on a few restful moments: reading the paper in bed at the weekend, lying down on the couch and listening to at least one song when he gets in from work, using bus journeys to listen to a podcast instead of checking his email, and making time to sit on a bench outside to eat his sandwich at lunchtime with a colleague, even if it is only for ten to fifteen minutes.

Jack has to schedule rest to make it happen, and the appointments with himself are the easiest thing for him to cancel, depriving him of these brief moments of rest in order to prioritize other people's needs or to fill up his time with busy stuff. The more he manages to keep a bit of space for rest, though, the better he feels. In fact, the more he craves it. He starts making sure one night a week is at home just chilling out. He begins to get sick a bit less often. He starts to have more space to think about how he wants things to be.

Having more space to think about how things are and how we want them to be is a good thing, but it can also be painful. Sometimes we stuff our time full of things so that we don't have to acknowledge the bits that are missing. For Jack, he begins to be aware that despite all his work colleagues and friends he feels quite lonely. This is really tough to recognize, and takes a bit of acknowledging, but it also means that he now has the choice to do something about it.

It's not just rest that Jack struggles with, it's also sleep. Rest without sleep is important, but sleep itself has its own unique benefits. A lack of sleep has been associated with poorer mental and physical health, although we know less about the mechanisms by which this happens. Shift work is now seen as an occupational hazard, though, as the impact on our mind and body of doing night shifts is understood more. Not only is it isolating to be operating at a different time to everyone else, but the change to our sleep cycle also seems to be detrimental to our health. Spare a thought here for new parents or people who are caring for sick loved ones too, who are often doing involuntary night shifts and muddling through.

Cycles are a feature, here again, of the experiences we have, both unconscious as well as conscious. In a night of sleep, we cycle through different sleep phases, from stage 1 to 4, with rapid eye movement (REM) sleep as part of this too. It's during REM sleep that we dream, and that we are more likely to wake up because we are sleeping more lightly.

We know that depriving humans and animals of sleep has negative effects on mental performance and physical health. Alarmingly, rats deprived of sleep actually die, although it's hard to disentangle the lack of sleep from the stress that they are under, since they aren't voluntarily choosing to have a lack of sleep and they don't understand why the conditions they are in are not letting them. Anyone who has experienced sleep deprivation will be able to vouch for the moodiness and difficulty making decisions or learning anything new which comes with it (hands up here with my frequently waking one-year-old). Theories of why we need sleep include thinking that it is necessary to consolidate memories and learning,[4] to restore the cells in our bodies and brains, and to reduce our energy expenditure.[5] Although this all sounds very plausible and even obvious, we still don't really know exactly how sleep does all this, or why it is so important in so many animals (with the odd exception, for example migrating birds).

For those of us not working (or caring) overnight, on more of a standard schedule, sleep can still be disrupted. Insomnia is one of the most frustrating things, with nights seeming to last for days not hours, as you clock-watch and work out how many hours of sleep you might actually get. Sleeplessness is frustrating, lonely and common. Approximately one in ten adults experience persistent and severe insomnia with daytime consequences, which means that 10 per cent of people find it hard to sleep on three or more nights a week and have had this problem for at least three months. In adults over sixty-five the figure rises dramatically, estimated as one in five. Lots of people experience sleep difficulties from time to time or to a less severe degree, so this really is a common problem.[6]

Simply put, insomnia is when sleep at night is not good and this affects how you feel the next day. It might be that it's hard to get to sleep, hard to stay asleep or both. The knock-on effects the following day can be sleepiness, irritability, teariness, poor performance at work or home, arguments with friends and family, and many more. So while insomnia can feel like a night-time problem, it really is a 24-hour disorder. The effects it has stretch well into the daytime and can make life feel miserable. Anxiety and low mood are common bedfellows of insomnia, and it's easy to see why: poor sleep tends to make us feel more emotionally reactive, and feeling more emotional, in particular sad or anxious, makes us sleep worse. Long-term sleep difficulties are associated with an increased likelihood of developing depression.

Sleep problems can result from multiple causes and trying to identify any longer-term factors, shorter-term triggers and accidental maintaining factors that keep the problem going can be helpful initial steps in working out what is going on. If there's something else in the context that is making sleep difficult then it makes sense to try to tackle that first. Sometimes fairly simple-seeming changes to the environment we are sleeping in, or the routine we have before bed, can make a big difference. Sometimes worries about other areas of our life are the problem, and then thinking about problem-solving or tackling those worries can help sleep get better. And sometimes we might just be running on adrenaline in the day, and finding it too hard to switch to a restorative state later on.

Thinking about how we prepare ourselves for sleep can help to set us up well, and remembering evidence-based strategies for getting back to sleep if we suffer from insomnia, including, counter-intuitively perhaps, getting up and doing something else for a bit instead of lying there clock-watching.

The idea that insomnia is something we can't change is one example of a thought about sleeplessness that might be unhelpful, as it might lead us to have a learned helplessness about the problem. Remember, we met learned helplessness in February's chapter, when we heard about those studies with the rats. It's when we stop trying to fix something, because we've tried a few times and nothing has worked. It's a state of mind associated with depression.

Racing thoughts at bedtime are another common problem. Often people lie awake chewing over things that have happened that day, trying to problem-solve dilemmas or just worrying about 'what ifs'. Alternatively, we might lie there overthinking our sleeplessness, worrying about what it will mean for us the next day, being hyper-alert to how our bodies feel, or thinking about how much we are thinking. It's easy to have catastrophic thoughts about sleeplessness, leading to feeling hopeless. Going to bed thinking, 'I'm going to be up all night', 'I won't be able to function at all tomorrow', 'This is a disaster', can put us in a tense frame of mind and make it harder to sleep. Similarly, clock-watching overnight, working out how many hours of sleep we will have left, is counterproductive, as it normally makes us more tense and less likely to drop off. Instead, try writing worries down in a notebook by the bed to leave the day behind before you go to sleep, or sidestepping problematic thoughts by using a podcast or relaxation track, or having some set phrases to remind yourself of, like 'I'm still managing to rest.'

There are also several things we can do to set ourselves up well for a good night's rest. Sleep hygiene refers to the basics of behaviour and environment that we can pay attention to in order to promote sleep. Lifestyle factors we engage in during the day can be important: for example, cutting down on caffeine, alcohol and nicotine, and trying to do some exercise but not too close to bedtime. Our routine just before bedtime is also important. CBT approaches recommend a wind-down routine sixty to ninety minutes before bed, and suggest that we pay attention to the comfort in our bedroom: noise, temperature, lighting, whether it's stuffy or not, and how comfy our bed and pillows are. Conversely, this does not mean that we try so hard to make a perfect bedtime routine that we end up piling the pressure on ourselves to sleep. Making sure our sleep pattern has a regular waking time and bedtime and doesn't involve napping is also useful, because often napping in the day means we don't sleep later and can end up in a vicious cycle. On the other hand, for some people, paradoxical interventions like trying to stay awake can have the effect of taking the pressure off sleep to an extent that it becomes easier.

Behaviours in the bedroom are also important. We need to associate our bed with sleep, which means not playing on our iPads, doing work, or chatting on the phone (sex is allowed!). If we can't sleep for longer than fifteen minutes the recommendation is to get up. If we lie there stewing for hours we will associate our bed with sleeplessness. Instead, we should get up and go into another room – read, make a hot drink or a hot-water bottle, write some pages of a journal, something low-activity (and preferably not involving looking at a screen) that won't make us feel really awake but will allow us to go back to bed when we start to feel sleepy again.

What if sleep just isn't possible for whatever reason? Does having a good rest count just as much? Unfortunately, much of the evidence suggests not, but I still think it is better than nothing. Yoga nidra, a type of yoga which involves taking deep rest in relaxing, long poses, is a practice which encourages the body and mind to slow down, again helping the parasympathetic nervous system to be activated. Even small micro-opportunities for rest and relaxation can sometimes help, as my wise yoga teacher, Marinella, is very good at reminding her classes. A three-minute mindfulness exercise can reset the way we are approaching things. A quiet cup of tea outside can give us a bit of breathing space for our mind. A short walk from our desk to get a sandwich at lunchtime can help us to switch off from the whir of our brains at work. Take your rest where you can get it, basically.

For Jack, his psychiatrist-training hours mean he is intermittently on night shifts, and there is nothing he can do about that. He can control some other aspects of his evenings, though. He starts to try what he routinely advises his own patients to do: not drinking coffee late in the day, not bingeing on his phone just before sleeping, trying to have the lights in his flat lower for a bit and do something relaxing just before bed. It's often surprising how much following the advice we give others can be helpful for ourselves.

Just as trying to do too many things is a repeating pattern that Jack (and many of the rest of us) get into, you will have yours as well. It doesn't mean we are backsliding, or back at square one, or a rubbish person, if we keep finding ourselves in the same pattern. It just means we are human. Perfectly imperfect. Continually being offered new opportunities to practise what we have learnt, and very often missing those opportunities and learning the same lessons over (and over) again.

I hope you can see this chapter as an invitation to try to stop and appreciate any chance to rest that you have. However small, however insignificant it might feel, those moments of stopping, savouring, and maybe even sleeping, can help November feel like a cosy cocoon instead of a claustrophobic, miserable month. Embracing the chance to rest can make all the difference.

VALUING REST

Key Ideas

1. If you're overstressed, try to work out what's in your control or not – and problem-solve and make changes to the bits you can.

2. Joy can compensate for lack of rest. Build in moments of joy even if your schedule is busy. It can be something super-short – a ten-minute call with a friend, a really good coffee – but something pleasurable each day.

3. Don't ignore your body's signals that it needs a rest: it's your immune system working – it's a good thing.

4. Set aside some time to look ahead and plan soothing activities and rest periods, even short ones: a three-minute mindfulness break, a ten-minute walk in the park at lunchtime, or a quiet bath in the evening.

5. Ultimately rest is as important as action: it might help to see it as an action in itself.

6. If you are struggling to sleep, have a think about the thoughts you have about sleep, and how useful they are – if you need to, try dumping them in a journal before bed.

7. Think about the behaviours you use to help yourself sleep too, and how you might be able to tweak these. Small changes made consistently can have a big impact.

8. Stop clock-watching and get up for a bit if you're lying there stewing. You can always make tea and go back to bed.

9. If you want to read more on sleep, Colin Espie's book *Overcoming Insomnia and Sleep Problems* is a good one.

12

DECEMBER

It's Christmas

Negotiating Families and
Managing Expectations

Have you ever been to Paris?

I lived in Paris for a year in my early twenties. I moved there with my good friend Katie to teach English, just after university when we didn't know what we really wanted to do and it seemed like a good idea to not know what to do in a different country instead of at home.

It was a good idea, and it made the usual difficulties of our early twenties (dating, hangovers, how to save enough money for the electricity bill, how to decide what to do with our life) feel somehow more romantic and dramatic against the backdrop of a whole new city in a whole new country.

For me Paris will always be a beautiful place, crammed with the foreign thrill of people speaking French, tiny bars, street art, hidden squares and dark, cosy cafés. The particular smell of the hot air in the Métro, the bakeries selling amazing bread and croissants on nearly every corner, the style of the clothes that people wear as they go about their business – all of this feels like a source of delight to me.

Not everyone feels this way, though. There's a thing called Paris syndrome:[1] a rare city-specific problem first written about in the 1980s, where tourists get so disorientated by being in Paris that they become panicked and upset. It is linked with feelings of disappointment that the French capital isn't as they have seen in films and read about in novels. To be fair, Paris is not always like the soft-focus romantic scenes of it. It has a relentless amount of dog mess on the pavements, which you never see in the films. There are Métro strikes nearly as often as there are not, and road rage which is continually dialled up. Coffees in central Paris are extortionately expensive, and waiters will give you side-eye if you mispronounce a word or get the masculine or feminine of its pronoun wrong. On a wintry day, corners of the city can feel as bleak as any other world capital, so despite my love of the place, I can see that Paris syndrome makes sense.

I think Christmas is a bit like Paris. The expectation, the pressure, and the feeling of melancholy when things don't land how they did in your imagination.

I'm thinking about Christmas in this chapter, but the ideas about expectation management and how to negotiate family gatherings might just as easily relate to other festivals this month, like Hanukkah or Kwanzaa, or to festivals at other times of the year.

The expectations we have of group celebrations, particularly Christmas, are often soft-focus rom-com, twinkling lights, gentle music in the background and a mulled wine on the go. Cosy, connected, calm. In reality, such celebrations are usually littered with potential stresses. The pressure to have a nice day, combined with an infrequent trip home or to see old friends, is a recipe for a row. Or the contrast between what we imagine everyone else to be having – the perfect *Waltons* Christmas – and whatever is *actually* going on for us: maybe a solo Christmas, or one with friends not family, or one where the tension over Christmas breakfast can be sliced with a knife, or one where we try frantically to see multiple family members who don't all get along, and end up dashing about, frazzled and knackered. My own experience of Christmas changed when my parents got divorced in my early twenties, and the logistics of working out where to be (and importantly with whom) seemed to loom large. My friend Laura negotiated this from an earlier age and refers to the changeover between parents as 'the exchange of prisoner', making a joke of the added layer of complexity which has to be navigated in families which may have parts in multiple locations.

So, public holidays can be a tricky time: family packed together at close quarters isn't always a recipe for happiness and harmony. Why are family relationships thrown into relief at these times and how can we get through it?

Whether we're at home or abroad a lot of the anguish can boil down to a conflict between expectations and reality, both for ourselves and others. It's one thing to feel sad, but a whole extra layer of pain if you're also beating yourself up about feeling sad because you think you should be happy.

The concept of radical acceptance can be useful here: accepting the reality of what is going on, even if it's painful. Radical acceptance is an idea which comes from dialectical behaviour therapy (which we met in August's chapter on managing anger). It doesn't mean we approve of something bad or even feel neutral about it, but it means we do accept what we can't change, even if we don't like it, rather than struggling against our current reality.

In some ways this is about control again. Control might lie internally (things which we can change) or externally, with the environment or other people (the stuff we can't change). There are always some things we do have control over in our lives, and just as we discussed in September's chapter in relation to work, focusing our energy on those things we can control, instead of the uncontrollable, can help us feel better. We can't always control family rituals or behaviours at Christmas, for example, but we can try to control how we respond to them, and what we plan to do. Similar principles can be useful at other times of year, whenever we're struggling with feeling out of control.

It can help to plan in advance, working out the bits we can control and how we want to do them. That might mean thinking through how to spend the day alone, doing your own thing with friends, or managing not to revert to fifteen-year-old behaviours if you choose to go home to your family. Taking a sidestep and considering the situation from other people's point of view can also help. What would create a different dynamic? Is there a different way of responding to others' needs while also meeting our own? And can we couple thinking about other perspectives with self-compassion?

Given how out of control anyone can feel at Christmas, it's maybe not surprising that it's such a busy time of year for mental health services. When I first worked in inpatient adolescent wards, before cuts to community services meant we were busy all year round, there tended to be noticeable peaks in the number of patient referrals at exam time, back-to-school time and Christmas time. And mostly, when I've been seeing someone for individual therapy around Christmas, we've spent time planning how to mitigate Christmas stress.

We all tend to have some ways of managing when we feel out of control, and sometimes these can tip into being unhelpful (like we thought about in September's chapter with the stress bucket). Sometimes on referral forms for inpatient services the referrer would have written that the person being referred was controlling, or had a controlling parent. This always made me feel annoyed on the person's behalf, because the truth is that we are all controlling; we all want to feel that we are steering our own course through our life, relationships, and the general mess of being a living, breathing, feeling human.

Eating disorders and self-harm are two problems which can ramp up around Christmas, and although these might seem like extremes of behaviour, they're maybe not so far removed from some of the ways we all cope, so I think we can all learn a lot from the therapy used to tackle them.

Think about the run-up to Christmas and what comes to mind? Christmas lights, relentless advertising and panic buying of turkeys, trimmings and massive boxes of chocolates. Christmas is so food-focused that it's unsurprising eating disorders can get much worse at this time of year. The pressure of sitting down to eat at a big, long, meal, where family tensions are crawling around the table and comments on what you are eating are rife, can be unbearable if there are already stresses in your life about food.

Eating disorders are both about and not about the food, though. In therapy for eating disorders clear expectations of what is healthy to eat and monitoring of weight are part of the treatment, but individual therapy is much more about trying to grow the parts of someone's identity that the eating disorder has taken over, and reminding the sufferer of what the downsides might be to letting thoughts about calories take over. We don't have to be battling with an eating disorder to consider what parts of our identity get eclipsed by worry and bad behaviour at Christmas, and to ask ourselves which bits we want to try to hold on to despite all the stress and noise.

One of the most effective treatments for eating disorders includes working with the person's family as well as the individual. Family therapy for eating disorders tries to help people look at what their individual relationship with food is doing to the relationships with the people around them. Eating disorders often make other people in the family micro-manage what someone is eating, or give other family members the feeling of being hugely disempowered – maybe reflecting what the individual with the eating disorder is feeling themselves. The eating disorder can coax people into specific roles in a powerful way, a way which is hard to step out of.

Even when eating disorders are not around, we often tend to fall into familiar family roles at Christmas time. This often happens in a kind of domino effect, where someone in our family who always behaves in a certain way might then bring out a certain sympathetic role in us, even if we don't like it. So, if someone tends to be very talkative then it might make you withdraw, or conversely if someone is silent you might find yourself chatting on and on. In families we are often given labels: the quiet one, the flirty one, the serious one, the joker... If our family is used to seeing us as one of these then it can be hard to be seen as having any other characteristics, and we can feel a pressure to act in the same way even if we feel different. We can't control what someone else does, or how someone else sees us, but we can work to control what we do in response. Sometimes if we play with doing the opposite to what we naturally would fall into doing, then it can coax something different out of the other person. If someone always provokes a row with you, what would happen if you made a joke instead, or sidestepped the row? You might be surprised.

Multi-family systemic therapy for eating disorders is a type of therapy which involves several families at once, having therapeutic conversations about the eating disorders which their young people are experiencing.[2] Parents and children might split into different groups for a bit and share experiences, or siblings might have the chance to speak to other siblings. Children might swap parents for a lunchtime to see what happens when the parents are looking after someone else's child, and this is often interesting. Both parents and children can often see the perspective of children or parents from another family in a more sympathetic way. Children might eat more for the parents who aren't their own, and parents might be able to speak more calmly when they're advocating this with another couple's child.

Perhaps there's something to be learnt from this by the rest of us too. It depends who is there on Christmas Day, but sometimes, if we're going back to our family of origin, we slip into speaking in ways that we wouldn't if we had someone witnessing it, or in ways that we wouldn't to someone else's family member. Why is it OK to be so much ruder to our own? What would happen if we thought about what our family members might like with the same care applied to a family we knew less well? Trying to see things from someone else's perspective frees us up from our own head a bit as well. If we're thinking about making the day nice for someone else, we might be less invested in it being a certain way for us, which can help shake some of that Christmas expectation. Studies of general wellbeing at Christmas show that people tend to feel worse at this time of year, with one exception. Followers of Christianity tend to feel happier.[3] Maybe it's because there's a higher spiritual meaning that can be tapped into, again helping people to sidestep their own expectations and think about the needs of others and the meaning of the day with a wider lens.

I'm often astounded by how much people manage to accomplish in therapy, and in multi-family therapy I've seen families run with the lightest of prompts, and create important conversations about what their family relationships are like. Therapy conversations are like wedding speeches – we don't really have these heartfelt and amazing conversations day to day in families, maybe because it's too hectic, maybe because it's too risky, but it's often all there under the surface, and why wait to say the good stuff? In particular, at times when we feel disconnected from family members or disempowered in family situations, trying to make the effort to say what we really feel, in a way in which others are able to hear it, can pay dividends.

Another multi-family therapy exercise involves each family thinking about what would sum them up in a family crest. This can strengthen the story of the individuals as a group, helping them to negotiate the presence of an eating disorder with a stronger sense of their collective strengths or superpowers and a greater sense of togetherness. There doesn't need to be an eating disorder present to think about what a family's attributes are. No matter what has gone on in a family (and I truly believe there is no such thing as a 'normal' family), each one has particular strengths and often a particular sense of humour about their family identity. What would your family shield be?

If you're reading this thinking your family shield would be a broken mess of some kind or another, which you want to avoid, that's OK too. Just because Christmas is a time of traditions doesn't mean we have to stick to the same unhelpful ones year after year. If you know your family tradition is that everyone drinks too much and has a massive messy row, then that might be something you want to steer clear of. Maybe you want to grieve the reality, before then thinking about a new way of doing things. What is a new tradition, just for yourself, that you could put in its place? Maybe it's a solo tradition, a promise to yourself of a sliver of time to do something you care about. Maybe it's the promise of a new boundary, the chance to do something totally different.

Doing something different when we're used to doing things in a certain way can be tricky, especially if the thing we usually do has felt like it was helpful (even if it maybe wasn't). Self-harm is one such example – it is anything someone does to hurt themselves on purpose, usually as a way of managing big emotions. This might feel far removed from day-to-day life but let's take a minute to think about it. Consider Jo, who uses self-harm in different ways. She describes feeling an overwhelming avalanche of different emotions all at once, and using self-harm to punctuate these somehow, even though she then ends up feeling mostly guilty and ashamed. She sometimes feels numb and discon-nected, and uses self-harm to feel something again, even though this is often sadness. Jo is aware of how she uses this coping strategy, and mostly she doesn't want to be using it. It's the most effective shortcut she has in the moment for managing those overwhelming feelings or those absences of feeling, though, and so it's a tough habit to kick.

We might not all use behaviours that we would think of as self-harm to manage our emotions, and we might not all be unlucky enough to experience the scale of feeling that Jo is having to cope with, but I think we all engage in behaviours that are counterproductive sometimes.

Whether it's spending too much money, eating too much chocolate, drinking too much alcohol, or working too many hours, there's usually something we do that helps us manage feelings that we find difficult in the short term, but that might not be so great for us in the medium to long term (like we thought about in September with the stress bucket). Sometimes it can be what we don't do: ignoring a problem because it feels too hard to deal with and allowing it to persist.

Christmas is a time when emotions can run high, and it can be useful to be aware, like Jo is, of the traps we might fall into when we're trying to cope but which actually might instead trip ourselves up. Are we likely to drink too much on Christmas Day because we're nervous about a family dynamic, and is this likely to backfire in a messy row? Are we likely to try to cram too many social things in, and end up running from one thing to another and enjoying none of them? Are we at risk of eating absent-mindedly because we're bored or anxious, and then feeling bad about it afterwards? Or texting our ex happy Christmas and watching the phone for hours to see when they reply? Or needling a family member to have an argument because it feels inevitable on some level? Pick your poison: we've all got something we do as an unhelpful way of coping, often on autopilot. And at Christmas, when everyone tends to be stuck indoors together, we might find ourselves all doing our own unhelpful coping strategy at once.

Happily, the strategies we use in therapy to deal with self-harm[4] can be useful to know about for these other unhelpful coping strategies too.

When people come to therapy for self-harm they might be at different stages of wanting to make a change. Many of the young people I have met while working in acute mental health wards were initially pretty sure they didn't want to stop self-harming; it was one of the few things making them feel better. It had often got them into an impossible situation, though, where everyone around them was desperate for them to make a shift and with time and reflection they could also see some problems with it.

Whatever the context and whatever the level of motivation to change, it is often helpful to begin in a similar way: trying to make sense together of what is going on and why. I am a big fan of keeping this as simple as possible, and I often use a general outline of thinking about what's happening. This includes 'what's going on?' – the problems that are bringing someone to therapy; 'why me?' – any history which has made the problems more likely; 'why now?' – any triggers that have set things off; 'why still?' – any things which are accidentally keeping the problem going; and 'what helps?' – things the person has already found helpful. Hopefully throughout the time I meet with someone we will expand the 'what helps?' until there are loads of tools that the person can draw upon.

A next step is often one borrowed from motivational interviewing (which we touched on briefly way back in January). Motivational interviewing is an approach used a lot in addiction services, developed in the 1980s by William R. Miller from Norway and his colleague Stephen Rollnick.[5] Miller and Rollnick developed a way of working with people experiencing addiction which shifted from advising people what to do, to trying to get alongside someone and letting them explore the pros and cons of their behaviour for themselves. One exercise they used was thinking together with someone about the short-term and long-term pros and cons of a behaviour. This seemingly simple exercise can be hugely powerful, if the ideas are coming from the person seeking help rather than being foisted on to them. It links a little with the stages of change that we thought about in February's chapter too, where we may or may not be quite ready to make a shift, and this readiness might fluctuate over time.

Let's use these ideas to think about Jo. Jo is using self-harming as a way of managing overwhelming feelings, and also as a way of making herself feel something when she feels numb or empty. She has been through some difficult things in her life, including tricky relationships with her parents which sometimes leave her feeling that her feelings aren't valid. She has a stressful job, and when things get very stressy at work it tends to trigger thoughts of being an imposter. She finds it hard to read her colleagues' opinions of her, and often experiences them as disliking her, even when they don't. On the other hand, sometimes one of her colleagues is objectively insulting and unsupportive, but she finds it hard to challenge this directly. On top of this she has a volatile romantic relationship and she has been turning to self-harm when work stress and romantic rows collide. Although self-harm helps in the short term, she finds herself feeling disgusted soon afterwards, and she is finding it hard to hide self-harm from her partner, which is another source of shame.

Jo wants to have some ways of managing other than self-harm, and when she draws out the pros and the cons of self-harm this is confirmed. For self-harm to be an ongoing problem there must be some perceived pay-off: people don't engage in something repeatedly if there's nothing in it for them. For Jo, pay-off is the sense of either relief from her mess of feelings, or the sense of coming back to reality from being disconnected, and these are powerful motivations. The downsides are more numerous, though: she doesn't want to have to explain her self-harm scars to anyone; she wants to be able to wear short-sleeved tops in the summer without worrying; and she doesn't want to be stuck with the guilty, shameful feelings afterwards. She wants to feel like she has 'adult' ways of managing, which help her to feel more in control, not less. She writes these things down; there's something about writing things down in your own handwriting that helps it go in a bit more and feel more solid.

There's nothing to stop any of us using this pros-and-cons approach for whatever our unhelpful coping strategies are. Instead of beating ourselves up, what are the helpful and unhelpful bits of what we do? Does this change when we think about the consequences short term and medium to long term? Will a three-day hangover spoil the only holiday we've had for ages, for example? Will a row with our mum leave us feeling rubbish for a week? Is the fallout worth it? Doing this in advance, before we need to use whichever strategy we tend to rely on, helps us to be able to plan whether we want to avoid it.

Jo has already tried some alternatives to self-harm. In fact, she has tried a lot of things, and lots of them haven't helped. One or two things have helped, though, and she is also up for experimenting with other stuff she hasn't tried. In between therapy sessions she has a go at some other strategies and finds a couple extra to add to her repertoire. She doesn't need all the alternatives to work, she just needs a few things that do.

It's the same for anyone: you don't need a million and one alternative ways of managing. You actually only need one, or maybe optimally a few more so you feel like you have a range of techniques at your disposal. Common ideas to try to soothe ourselves often use the five senses – hearing, smell, taste, touch and sight – to calm or ground us. Alternatively, especially if someone is feeling disconnected, they might use the senses to surprise or shock them into feeling something. So, a strong taste or smell, or a strong sensation (like holding an ice cube, or putting your face in cold water), can help to get us into a slightly different state of mind. What works depends on what the function is of the behaviour you are trying to shift. So if the unhelpful behaviour is being used to provide relief for huge emotions, then other things that do that might be helpful – having a big shout, writing in a journal, going for a run. If the unhelpful behaviour is being used to feel more connected, then strong sensations or practices which help someone feel grounded in their body might be more effective: ice-cold water or sniffing a powerful smell.

Now, even if we have some alternatives that are more useful than the unhelpful behaviour we are used to, it doesn't mean we will find them easy to put into practice, especially if we have a habitual response which is our typical pattern. For Jo, she works hard at setting up reminders in advance to help her practise the stuff that might make self-harm less likely. The reminders are about how to keep doing stuff that releases pressure ahead of things feeling so full on that she feels overwhelmed or disconnected. These are things like deep breathing, relaxation strategies, time to herself at regular intervals, even if it is just a minute in the loo. She also considers the idea of what 'roadblocks' she might use if she feels about to self-harm. The roadblocks are more about ways of stopping herself if self-harm is really imminent: things like looking at a picture of her and her friends on her phone and remembering she didn't want to have to hide her self-harm from them, making sure she stayed near to other people so that she was less likely to self-harm, and reminding herself that she could do this – that she'd already gone however many days without self-harming.

For all of us, if there are behaviours we really want to avoid over Christmas, then it's worth planning ahead and thinking about what will take the pressure off during the run-up and the day itself. We only do Christmas once a year and often it's different each time, so it's not like it's a day we are practised at, but we can practise ways of releasing stress before it gets too much, and ways of putting in roadblocks to whatever our unhelpful behaviours are.

An important part of working on self-harm, which can be applied to other self-sabotaging behaviours too, comes from solution-focused therapy,[6] although it has been embraced by other schools of therapy as well. It can easily get overlooked, but it's the idea of spotting progress, and amplifying it. Self-harm is never around 24/7, so what is going on when it's not around? What is helping it to stay at bay? Asking these questions suddenly flips things on their head and makes the conversation more about the huge swathes of time where people are coping really well, rather than the small amounts of time where it all feels too much.

Similarly, at Christmas, it's rare that the whole thing is a total disaster. What happens in the nice bits? And how can we grow them? If you think back to past Christmases, where things have gone well, how can you replicate that or increase it? Perhaps it was something thoughtful you did for someone else that made you feel really good. Maybe it was the journey taken to travel between two family members' homes which gave you a chance to sing along to your favourite music. Maybe it was keeping things simple in some way. Perhaps it was something seemingly small, like popping out for a brief walk at some point or having a nap. Whatever helped, think about how you can have that plan up your sleeve. And try to celebrate the things that are going well. It doesn't have to be the most amazing Christmas for it to be worth celebrating. Maybe it's just good enough, and for the majority of it you haven't fallen into the bear traps you wanted to avoid. That's great. Even if you did fall in one of them. That's just human and you are probably doing better than you think. In the end, just as we thought about at the start of this book when we considered New Year's Eve, Christmas is just another day. I'm wishing you a good one, though.

NEGOTIATING FAMILIES AND MANAGING EXPECTATIONS

Key Ideas

1. Beware the expectation gap at Christmas. There's nothing wrong with hoping things will be a certain way, but if they go differently take a deep breath and try to practise acceptance of how things really are, rather than getting hung up on the gap between your imagination and reality.

2. Think in advance about what you can control and what you can't. You can't control what other people do. You can control your reaction. It might help to plan for worst-case scenarios so you know what you'll do if a family row blows up or if you feel miserable for some reason. Work out your coping strategies. It can also help to think about bits that have usually gone well. How can you amplify those things this year? Are there things you want to repeat?

3. You can also control your boundaries, even if it doesn't always feel like it. Planning in advance what you are happy with doing or not doing, and how to gracefully say what you want, can also help.

4. This doesn't mean you have to ignore what other people want. Thinking about Christmas from other people's perspective can help it go better too, and give you the positive feeling you get from doing nice things for others.

5. Trying to shift perspective to take a wider-lens view is another idea. What is Christmas about for you? Connection with people you love? A spiritual experience? A chance to have a rest? An opportunity to make time for something you prioritize, like creativity or learning? What is the underlying value you want this Christmas to embody? How can you keep that in mind? And remember it's fine to swerve all the previous traditions and create your own.

6. Think about the roles you get invited to play in your family or social group. Are you happy with them? If you want to shift things, try experimenting with something else: acting the opposite of what people expect, or leaving space for someone else to step into what you usually do.

7. Think about the pros and cons of the strategies you normally use to help manage stressful times, and work out whether these are helpful for you or not. If you want to change them, experiment with alternatives in advance, and think about what your 'roadblocks' could be to remind yourself to do something differently.

8. If it all goes to pot, be gentle with yourself. Christmas can be intense. A row or the use of an unhelpful coping strategy doesn't mean that all is lost. Try to take time to calm down and regroup, and speak to yourself in the way you would to a good friend. You've not blown it.

EPILOGUE

Well, here we are at the end of the year, and also, of course, nearly at the beginning again. I'm going to recap some of what we've thought about each month, before I take this opportunity to say a little more about the writing of this book and my hopes and wishes for you, the reader.

We began our adventure together in January, when we thought about the start of the year, that invitation to be a fresh new you, and the pressure that comes with this. We thought about how to make decisions and changes in our lives, whether big or small, and how hard this can be. Things that helped ranged from trying to make decisions earlier in the day, writing pros and cons lists and using our values as a compass, to remembering that decisions are hard and change is tiring, and trying to be kind to ourselves in the midst of it all, since anxiety and loss often accompany transitions. We touched on the repetitive thinking styles of worry and rumination, and how labelling these when we spot them can be useful in sidestepping the unhelpful thought spirals they encourage us to slide down.

In February we thought about getting unstuck when it's dreary outside and feels hard to get going. We thought about how doing things before we feel like it can make us feel more in the mood for action. We thought about trying to savour times we feel pleasure or a sense of pride in what we've done. We thought about taking small steps towards things we feel anxious about, or towards things that matter to us. We noticed how some of what January's chapter covered on using our values can be useful for when we're feeling stuck too – reorienting our personal compass to feel like we know why we are pointing in a certain direction. We also thought about how comparisons with other people can sometimes get us stuck in a rut because we feel like we're not doing enough, but we're all doing things at our own pace, and it's important not to compare our worst day with someone else's best day and then feel bad.

In March we did some spring-cleaning. Borrowing some of the ideas from therapeutic spaces, we thought about tweaks we can make at home or at work to make us feel calmer and happier. The different senses all have something to offer, especially in helping us to calm our nervous systems down. Making the most of natural light, and natural materials like wood, as well as trying to bring nature inside with house plants and scenic views (even just a picture) help us to feel better. The balance between feeling safe and cosy and feeling a sense of surprise or mystery can help us make the most of our spaces, and having flexible spaces which allow sociability as well as privacy can also be beneficial. Reducing clutter, by considering whether we really want or need objects around us, can help us to feel calmer in ourselves as well as giving us a clear surface or two.

In April the blossoming trees got us thinking about how we nourish ourselves and encourage our own blossoming.

How we talk to ourselves is important and trying to change a critical inner monologue can be powerful. Noticing when we have a go at ourselves and trying to change the tone of voice or the content of what we say can help, and thinking about what we would say to a good friend is a nice prompt to use. We thought about remembering that we are all human and all experience suffering sometimes, but bringing ourselves back to the here and now and trying to connect with ourselves in this moment can be steadying. If we're jumping to conclusions about how nasty other people or the world is, then having a reality check and looking for evidence for and against these beliefs is beneficial. We thought about externalizing our inner critic to make it really separate from us, and we used ideas from narrative therapy to remember that we do have some control over how we join the dots together in our own stories.

In May spring really is in full swing, and we might be turning outwards more to interact with people around us. We thought about the art of talking and listening, using some of the ideas that therapeutic conversations can offer to enhance conversations in all areas of life. Using open questions instead of closed ones, stopping and taking time to properly listen instead of multitasking and checking that we've understood by summarizing back, can all help us to be more present in a dialogue. Being brave enough to leave a silence sometimes, and commenting on the process of a conversation, can sometimes get us to hidden depths we might not have been aware of. We thought about assertiveness skills in conversations too, and how to have a good row which involves creative problem-solving instead of blame or the same old patterns that we can fall into. Trying to keep communication going, no matter in which medium, is sometimes the most we can think about, and sometimes just enough.

In June we thought about feeling connected to others, in this social time of weddings and parties and long summer nights. We thought about things that can get in the way of connection, like social anxiety, or misunderstandings, or repeating patterns from previous relationships. We thought about ways to overcome these obstacles, like shifting our focus from ourselves on to who and what is around us, trying to spot repeating patterns and doing things slightly differently, and being more explicit about what we mean and what we think someone else means. These things can help in all sorts of connections, from romantic to friendships to family to work colleagues, but ultimately the relationship we have with ourself underpins all of these, and it's worth spending time to take care of ourselves so that we feel that we have enough energy to give to others too.

In July we thought about existential angst and uncertainty, how to tolerate it and reduce it. We thought about being careful with our information diet, not doom-scrolling or over-researching unanswerable questions. We also thought about giving ourselves a sense of safety through small rituals day to day and training our attention on the here and now. Sifting through what is under our control and what is not can help to guide us towards what might be helpful to plan and what might not. Through it all we can try to hold ourselves gently: life is full of uncertainties and it's difficult.

In the heat of August we thought about managing red-hot anger. Not by squashing it, but by trying to understand if there are other feelings accompanying it which need some attention, or if anger is signalling to us about something else which needs to be done. Instead of getting caught up in angry thoughts, using perspective shifts like zooming out or zooming forward in time, practising mindfulness and naming the emotions that are passing through, and taking care of our bodies so we are not acting from a point of depletion, can all help. Dialectical behaviour therapy skills like assertiveness, self-soothing and acting the opposite were also in the mix as things to try if anger risks overwhelming our mind and behaviour.

In September, with its back-to-school vibe, we thought about work and how to minimize that Sunday night dread. That balance cropped up again, of what we can control and what we can't, and tweaking our job using job crafting to make it the best it can be for us was one idea we thought about. We noticed how perfectionism can sometimes be unhelpful and identified simple ways to overcome this, and we thought about how working out what's in our stress bucket and what might punch holes in it can be a nice template for daily self-care. Mindfulness was here again, as a way of managing stress at work, and so was thinking about how we talk to colleagues about traumatic information, if our jobs involve that. We thought about trying to remember the good stuff too: there must be a reason why we're in the job we are, but sometimes we can forget to celebrate the positive bits. If there's not enough to celebrate we might be mulling over leaving, in which case thinking about endings can help with the process of going.

In October we thought about other types of endings, those involved in the losses we all experience throughout our lives. Loss is hard to talk about, and there's no right way or wrong way to experience loss and grief, but thinking about how to balance mourning and reconnection can help, as can thinking about how we want to honour a memory or a grief, to keep someone or something alive in a different way. There are all sorts of ways to do this, and finding our own traditions can be part of what is helpful.

In November we considered resting. Why it matters, how to do it more, and what to do if we can't do it too. Sleep was part of this, making sure we're doing what we can to optimize it, but beyond sleep there are other types of rest as well, and even tiny pockets of rest throughout the day can make a big difference. Ultimately, rest is just as important as action. It might help us to see it as an action in itself.

Our final chapter in December was about Christmas and the family negotiations and expectation management that can come along with this festive season. We thought about minding the expectation gap between the fairy lights and rom-coms and the reality of the Christmas break. We considered how to approach our families with a fresh perspective, and how to plan for what is under our control and let go of some of what isn't, thinking about how to change what we do which is unhelpful even if it feels like it helps in the moment. Being gentle with ourselves at this time of year (and all year) is important.

I hope the book has been useful to you, and that it might continue to be a resource that you can dip into if you want to remind yourself of some of the tips and tricks from what psychological therapies can offer. It's no substitute for actually having therapy, but you might not feel like you need therapy, and the ideas can still be useful to think about outside of the therapy room. Just as there is a spectrum of experience with mental health, so there is a spectrum of uses for therapy and psychological knowledge. Sometimes we might use some ideas with a light touch, sometimes we might decide to go all in and seek professional help for a particular difficulty. Whichever, I strongly believe that these ideas are helpful and should be shared around as much as possible. Life can be tricky and it's good to have tools to help us manage. The notes pages will give you some of the sources I've referred to, and I've also tried to signpost in the key ideas some of the self-help texts which can be useful if you're feeling stuck on the things covered in a particular chapter.

If you do decide to seek therapeutic help, I'd recommend speaking to your GP and also doing your own research on which type of therapy would be most beneficial for whichever concern you are hoping to address. In the UK the NICE guidelines (which are available online)[1] review and summarize the evidence for different approaches for different diagnoses, if you know that a particular diagnosis is relevant for you. It might also help to read up a little on what the different types of therapy are like to see which you like the feel of, especially if more than one type of therapy is recommended for the problem you are seeking help for, or also if you feel like you would benefit from some sessions of therapy in a more exploratory way rather than to tackle something in particular. Hopefully the previous chapters give you a bit of a flavour of some different types of therapy. The final chapter of a former book I wrote (*Blueprint: How Our Childhood Makes Us Who We Are*) also goes through different types of therapeutic approach if you want to read a bit more. You can also search for the webpage of the professional body of the therapy you are interested in to explore further, and these websites often signpost how you can make sure you find an appropriately qualified therapist, if you are seeking help privately. (In the UK, NHS therapists have their qualifications checked, but you can also always ask them what they are.)

When I was writing this book I thought about decisions (and some mistakes!) which I've made throughout my life so far, and thought about the advice which I would give my younger self now. Or maybe also my older self, because we are all human, and we learn through making repeated mistakes, often. Life is a messy old business, but also a beautiful one.

All of the advice which I can glean from therapy, some of which I have tried to share with you here, is something I try to practise myself, and continually fall short of mastering. I find the principles helpful nonetheless, and I enjoy reflecting on the ways in which psychology can shed light on life's happenings and human behaviours, with a view always to try to learn what can be learnt, even if I don't always succeed in using it in every moment. It's never failing to have to learn something again, or to find ourselves falling in and out of the same dilemmas. It's just being human and going round again, but hopefully with a different perspective each time.

I pitched the idea for this book while I was pregnant and then wrote it on maternity leave. I have written it in a different way to how I ever wrote before. Where previously I would have used writing retreats and gone off for a week at a time to write thousands of words at once, for this book I've written in shorter bursts, when possible.

It's been a different sort of writing and maybe a different sort of thinking too – which may have particularly suited this project with its structure of a year. This year I have been very tuned into the small changes which happen daily with a young baby, and which really are quite big changes as well. I've spent a lot of time walking around with my son in a sling, showing him leaves and flowers as they arrive, and time too watching him go from immobile with a jelly-like neck to a crawling, then standing, then walking person with clear ideas of where he wants to go.

I finished the first draft of the book just as he turned one, and thinking back over the first year of motherhood, which has been very different to any of the years that have gone before, I still recognize the ebb and flow of the cycles and seasons, which continue just as they have always done. Even in times of uncharted territory in our lives, no matter what we are struggling with or rejoicing in, we have those familiar seasonal milestones. Cycles are continuously going on around us as well as within us.

The year, and life in general, is full of repeating patterns, and fresh starts. In amongst this, the dialectics that we touched upon in August's chapter, those conflicting truths which simultaneously coexist, are woven into our daily experiences. We may strive to do things differently at the same time as repeating many mistakes we hope to avoid. We may confront impossible dilemmas, difficult moments and challenging conversations at the same time as encountering deep joy, simple pleasures, moments of connection and chances for growth. All of these things can be true at once.

For all that there are repeating patterns, just as we acknowledged in January's and July's chapters, we have no idea what is going to happen next, as much as we may long to. We can't know, and maybe we don't need to. Trying to stay in the present moment but appreciate the resonances with what has gone before, and with what the psychological literature can teach us, can be grounding. Whatever it is that you hold dear to you in your life, and whichever values are yours, I hope an occasional pause and moment of reflection can allow you to feel like you are the shore that the waves come back to, rather than the boat which is tossed upon them. And I hope the odd idea or two from this book might lodge somewhere and be useful at some of these times.

Acknowledgements

Writing a book is a funny old business. It's a lovely old business too, and I've felt very grateful for the impetus to carve out time to reflect on and write about these ideas. A large number of people are involved in making any book happen, and this one is no exception. I would like to say some thank yous here.

Publishing a book is a huge process that takes much longer than just the writing. Thank you to Kate Barker, my agent, for your belief in the idea to begin with and encouragement to use my own voice, and for your support throughout. The professional and friendly team at Atlantic Books have been great. Thank you Ed Faulkner, for your acceptance of the pitch and your enthusiasm and helpful edits. Thank you Kate Ballard, for your thoughtful edits which made my writing sound better but still like my own, and for your gentle tone of feedback which made the editing process much more enjoyable. Thank you to the wider team at Atlantic Books too: Niccolò De Bianchi who worked on production, Kirsty Doole on publicity, Aimee Oliver-Powell on marketing, Dave Woodhouse and Patrick Hunter on selling to UK retailers, and Gemma Davis on selling to overseas outlets for export territories. Out of house several talented freelancers were involved: Mark Ecob designed the cover, Sarah-Jane Forder copy-edited the manuscript, Richard Rosenfeld proofread the final version and Ed Pickford did the typesetting.

More personally, I couldn't have written this without the support of my partner, Tim, both for stepping in to look after our son when I needed to write or to turn edits around, and for all the rest of the practical everyday things which you do to keep our family's wheels on. Thank you for your love and care and your beautiful illustrations for each chapter. Thank you also to my parents. To my mum, Barbara, for being deeply encouraging, reading early drafts and having interesting conversations about ideas; and to my dad, Piers, for your support in this strange year, for your interest in what I'm doing and for helping with some of the academic writing challenges which were going on at the same time.

Generous friends let me mention notes from our shared histories: thank you Katie, Laura, Anna and Chris. Thank you also to friends and clinical psychology colleagues Dr Rebecca Lockwood and Dr Jo Daniels, for reading early drafts of full or partial chapters on anger and loss respectively: I'm grateful for your helpful comments and reassurance. Any mistakes which remain are mine alone. Thanks to Dr Jane Gregory, too, for pointers to information on misophonia and to Marinella Benelli whose yoga classes added a new dimension to my thinking about rest.

Everything in this book comes from years of being able to work with wise colleagues and supervisors, and inspiring clients. I have continually learnt from the people who come to see me for therapy and the people who I have worked with in providing services, and I hope that I have done the ideas we have discussed justice.

Notes

1 January: Which Way Next?

1. Tyrer, P., and Baldwin, D. (2006), 'Generalized anxiety disorder', *Lancet*, 368(9553), 2156–66.
2. Ladouceur, R., Blais, F., Freeston, M. H., and Dugas, M. J. (1998), 'Problem solving and problem orientation in generalized anxiety disorder', *Journal of Anxiety Disorders*, 12(2), 139–52.
3. Dugas, M. J., Freeston, M. H., and Ladouceur, R. (1997), 'Intolerance of uncertainty and problem orientation in worry', *Cognitive Therapy and Research*, 21(6), 593–606.
4. Polman, E. (2012), 'Self–other decision-making and loss aversion', *Organizational Behavior and Human Decision Processes*, 119(2), 141–50.
5. Reynolds, D. B., Joseph, J., and Sherwood, R. (2009), 'Risky shift versus cautious shift: determining differences in risk taking between private and public management decision-making', *Journal of Business and Economics Research*, 7(1), 63–78.
6. Vohs, K. D., Baumeister, R. F., Schmeichel, B. J., Twenge, J. M., Nelson, N. M., and Tice, D. M. (2018), 'Making choices impairs subsequent self-control: a limited-resource account of decision-making, self-regulation, and active initiative', in Roy F. Baumeister, *Self-Regulation and Self-Control*, London, Routledge, pp. 45–77.

7. Danziger, S., Levav, J., and Avnaim-Pesso, L. (2011), 'Extraneous factors in judicial decisions', *Proceedings of the National Academy of Sciences*, 108(17), 6889–92.
8. Vohs et al., op. cit.
9. Spears, D. (2014), 'Decision costs and price sensitivity: field experimental evidence from India', *Journal of Economic Behavior and Organization*, 97, 169–84.
10. Chen, M. K., Lakshminarayanan, V., and Santos, L. (2005), 'The evolution of our preferences: evidence from capuchin monkey trading behavior', Cowles Foundation Discussion Paper, no. 1524, pp. 1–26.
11. Chen, M. K., Lakshminarayanan, V., and Santos, L. R. (2006), 'How basic are behavioral biases? Evidence from capuchin monkey trading behavior', *Journal of Political Economy*, 114(3), 517–37.
12. Watkins, E. R. (2008), 'Constructive and unconstructive repetitive thought', *Psychological Bulletin*, 134(2), 163.
13. Norcross, J. C., and Vangarelli, D. J. (1988), 'The resolution solution: longitudinal examination of New Year's change attempts', *Journal of Substance Abuse*, 1(2), 127–34.
14. Elliot, A. J., and Church, M. A. (1997), 'A hierarchical model of approach and avoidance achievement motivation', *Journal of Personality and Social Psychology*, 72(1), 218.
15. Prochaska, J. O., and DiClemente, C. C. (1982), 'Transtheoretical therapy: toward a more integrative model of change', *Psychotherapy: Theory, Research and Practice*, 19(3), 276.

2 February: Inching Forwards

1. Seligman, M. E. (1972), 'Learned helplessness', *Annual Review of Medicine*, 23(1), 407–12.
2. Veale, D. (2008), 'Behavioural activation for depression', *Advances in Psychiatric Treatment*, vol. 14, 29–36, doi: 10.1192/apt.bp.107.004051.

3. Jacobson, N. S., Dobson, K. S., Truax, P. A., et al. (1996), 'A component analysis of cognitive behavioral treatment for depression', *Journal of Consulting and Clinical Psychology*, 64, 295–304.
4. Dunn, B. D. (2012), 'Helping depressed clients reconnect to positive emotion experience: current insights and future directions', *Clinical Psychology and Psychotherapy*, 19(4), 326–40.
5. Furukawa, T. A., Imai, H., Horikoshi, M., Shimodera, S., Hiroe, T., Funayama, T., and FLATT investigators (2018), 'Behavioral activation: is it the expectation or achievement of mastery or pleasure that contributes to improvement in depression?', *Journal of Affective Disorders*, 238, 336–41.
6. Schumacher, S., Miller, R., Fehm, L., Kirschbaum, C., Fydrich, T., and Ströhle, A. (2015), 'Therapists' and patients' stress responses during graduated versus flooding *in vivo* exposure in the treatment of specific phobia: a preliminary observational study', *Psychiatry Research*, 230(2), 668–75.
7. https://www.sciencefocus.com/future-technology/phobias-paranoia-and-ptsd-why-virtual-reality-therapy-is-the-frontier-of-mental-health-treatment
8. Vogel, E. A., Rose, J. P., Roberts, L. R., and Eckles, K. (2014), 'Social comparison, social media, and self-esteem', *Psychology of Popular Media Culture*, 3(4), 206.

3 March: Spring Cleaning

1. Ulrich, R. S. (1984), 'View through a window may influence recovery from surgery', *Science*, 224(4647), 420–1.
2. Ulrich, R. S. (2002), 'Health benefits of gardens in hospitals', in *Plants for People International Exhibition Floriade*, vol. 17, no. 5, 2010.
3. Tse, M. M., Ng, J. K., Chung, J. W., and Wong, T. K. (2002), 'The effect of visual stimuli on pain threshold and tolerance', *Journal of Clinical Nursing*, 11(4), 462–9.

4. Lichtenfeld, S., Elliot, A. J., Maier, M. A., and Pekrun, R. (2012), 'Fertile green: green facilitates creative performance', *Personality and Social Psychology Bulletin*, 38(6), 784–97.
5. Friedman, R.S., and Forster, J. (2020), 'Implicit affective cues and attentional tuning: an integrative review', *Psychological Bulletin*, 136(5), 875.
6. Plambech, T., and Van den Bosch, K. (2015), 'The impact of nature on creativity – a study among Danish creative professionals', *Urban Forestry and Urban Greening*, I(14), 255–63.
7. Norwood, M. F., Lakhani, A., Maujean, A., Zeeman, H., Creux, O., and Kendall, E. (2019), 'Brain activity, underlying mood and the environment: a systematic review', *Journal of Environmental Psychology*, 65, 101321.
8. Some of the content of this chapter has been repurposed from my feature for Mosaic. You can read the original feature online here: https://mosaicscience.com/story/building-healthier-hospitals. I'd really recommend looking at the other articles too – Mosaic was a brilliant publication.
9. Walch, J. M., Rabin, B. S., Day, R., Williams, J. N., Choi, K., and Kang, J. D. (2005), 'The effect of sunlight on postoperative analgesic medication use: a prospective study of patients undergoing spinal surgery', *Psychosomatic Medicine*, 67(1), 156–63.
10. https://www.maudsleybrc.nihr.ac.uk/posts/2018/january/exposure-to-nature-in-cities-beneficial-for-mental-wellbeing
11. Danese, A., and Baldwin, J. R. (2017), 'Hidden wounds? Inflammatory links between childhood trauma and psychopathology', *Annual Review of Psychology*, 68, 517–44.
12. Morrison, R. L., and Macky, K. A. (2017), 'The demands and resources arising from shared office spaces', *Applied Ergonomics*, 60, 103–15.
13. Ibid.
14. Hirst, A. (2011), 'Settlers, vagrants and mutual indifference:

unintended consequences of hot-desking', *Journal of Organizational Change Management*, 24(6), 767–88.

15. Barrett, P., Zhang, Y., Moffat, J., and Kobbacy, K. (2013), 'A holistic, multi-level analysis identifying the impact of classroom design on pupils' learning', *Building and Environment*, 59, 678–89.

16. I talk with clinical psychologist and researcher Victoria Bream about this in this podcast episode: https://letstalkaboutcbt.libsyn.com/hoarding

17. Roster, C. A., Ferrari, J. R., and Jurkat, M. P. (2016), 'The dark side of home: assessing possession "clutter" on subjective wellbeing', *Journal of Environmental Psychology*, 46, 32–41.

4 April: Nourishing to Flourish

1. Koestner, R., Zuroff, D. C., and Powers, T. A. (1991), 'Family origins of adolescent self-criticism and its continuity into adulthood', *Journal of Abnormal Psychology*, 100(2), 191.

2. Jean Piaget wrote extensively about this and if you would like a summary there is a chapter about cognitive development in my book (2018), *Blueprint: How Our Childhood Makes Us Who We Are*, London, Robinson.

3. Freeman, D., Pugh, K., and Garety, P. (2008), 'Jumping to conclusions and paranoid ideation in the general population', *Schizophrenia Research*, 102(1–3), 254–60.

4. https://self-compassion.org

5. Morgan, A. (2000), *What Is Narrative Therapy?*, Adelaide, Dulwich Centre Publications, p. 116.

5 May: The Art of Talking (and Listening)

1. Roter, D. L., and Hall, J. A. (1987), 'Physicians' interviewing styles and medical information obtained from patients', *Journal of General Internal Medicine*, 2(5), 325–9.

2. Rogers, C. R., and Farson, R. (2021), *Active Listening*, Augusta GA, Mockingbird Press LLC, p. 4.
3. Notably cognitive behavioural therapy and dialectical behaviour therapy.
4. Speed, B. C., Goldstein, B. L., and Goldfried, M. R. (2018), 'Assertiveness training: a forgotten evidence-based treatment', *Clinical Psychology: Science and Practice*, 25(1), e12216.
5. Parr, P., Boyle, R. A., and Tejada, L. (2008), 'I said, you said: a communication exercise for couples', *Contemporary Family Therapy*, 30(3), 167–73.
6. Ahrens, C. E. (2006), 'Being silenced: the impact of negative social reactions on the disclosure of rape', *American Journal of Community Psychology*, 38(3), 263–74.

6 June: Summer Socializing

1. Keller, M. B. (2003), 'The lifelong course of social anxiety disorder: a clinical perspective', *Acta Psychiatrica Scandinavica*, 108, 85–94.
2. If you're interested in this, there is more in my book *Blueprint: How Our Childhood Makes Us Who We Are*.
3. https://mosaicscience.com/story/surviving-troubled-childhood-resilience-neglect-adversity
4. Bateman, A., and Fonagy, P. (2013), 'Mentalization-based treatment', *Psychoanalytic Inquiry*, 33(6), 595–613.

7 July: 3 a.m. Worries

1. Banks, J., Fancourt, D., and Xu, X. (2021), 'Mental health and the Covid-19 pandemic', in Helliwell, J. F., Layard R., Sachs J., and De Neve, J-E. (eds), *World Happiness Report 2021*, New York, Sustainable Development Solutions Network, 109–30.
2. Cullen, W., Gulati, G., and Kelly, B. D. (2020), 'Mental

health in the Covid-19 pandemic', *QJM: An International Journal of Medicine*, 113(5), 311–12.

3. Singh, S., Roy, D., Sinha, K., Parveen, S., Sharma, G., and Joshi, G. (2020), 'Impact of Covid-19 and lockdown on mental health of children and adolescents: a narrative review with recommendations', *Psychiatry Research*, 293, 113429.

4. Carleton, R. N., Desgagné, G., Krakauer, R., and Hong, R. Y. (2019), 'Increasing intolerance of uncertainty over time: the potential influence of increasing connectivity', *Cognitive Behaviour Therapy*, 48(2), 121–36.

5. Freeston, M., Tiplady, A., Mawn, L., Bottesi, G., and Thwaites, S. (2020), 'Towards a model of uncertainty distress in the context of coronavirus (Covid-19)', *Cognitive Behaviour Therapist*, 13, e31, 1–15.

6. For the podcast episode in which I interviewed Mark Freeston, visit https://letstalkaboutcbt.libsyn.com/tolerating-uncertainty-what-helps

7. Panu, P. (2020), 'Anxiety and the ecological crisis: an analysis of eco-anxiety and climate anxiety', *Sustainability*, 12(19), 7836.

8 August: Hot Under the Collar

1. Anderson, C. A. (2001), 'Heat and violence', *Current Directions in Psychological Science*, 10(1), 33–8.

2. Anderson, C. A., Bushman, B. J., and Groom, R. W. (1997), 'Hot years and serious and deadly assault: empirical tests of the heat hypothesis', *Journal of Personality and Social Psychology*, 73(6), 1213.

3. Dimeff, L., and Linehan, M. M. (2001), 'Dialectical behavior therapy in a nutshell', *California Psychologist*, 34(3), 10–13.

4. Yaden, David, Iwry, Jonathan, Slack, Kelley, Eichstaedt, Johannes, Zhao, Yukun, Vaillant, George, and Newberg, Andrew (2016), 'The overview effect: awe and

self-transcendent experience in space flight', *Psychology of Consciousness: Theory, Research, and Practice*, 3, 1–11.

5. Mischkowski, D., Kross, E., and Bushman, B. J. (2012), 'Flies on the wall are less aggressive: self-distancing "in the heat of the moment" reduces aggressive thoughts, angry feelings and aggressive behavior', *Journal of Experimental Social Psychology*, 48(5), 1187–91.

6. Bushman, B. J. (2002), 'Does venting anger feed or extinguish the flame? Catharsis, rumination, distraction, anger, and aggressive responding', *Personality and Social Psychology Bulletin*, 28(6), 724–31.

7. For an overview, this chapter by Bandura talks about his whole theory: Bandura, A. (2005), 'The evolution of social cognitive theory', in Smith, K. G. and Hitts, M. A. (eds), *Great Minds in Management*, Oxford, Oxford University Press, pp. 9–35.

8. Russo, M. A., Santarelli, D. M., and O'Rourke, D. (2017), 'The physiological effects of slow breathing in the healthy human', *Breathe*, 13(4), 298–309.

9 September: That Sunday Night Feeling

1. Spector, P. (1982), 'Behaviour in organizations as a function of employee's locus of control', *Psychological Bulletin* 91(3), 482–97.

2. Berg, J. M., Dutton, J. E., and Wrzesniewski, A. (2007), 'What is job crafting and why does it matter?', Centre for Positive Organizational Scholarship.

3. Wrzesniewski, A., and Dutton, J. E. (2001), 'Crafting a job: revisioning employees as active crafters of their work', *Academy of Management Review*, 26, 179–201.

4. Riley, C., and Shafran, R. (2005), 'Clinical perfectionism: a preliminary qualitative analysis', *Behavioural and Cognitive Psychotherapy*, 33(3), 369–74.

5. Shafran, R., Egan, S., and Wade, T. (2018), *Overcoming Perfectionism*, London, Robinson.

6. Bartlett, L., Martin, A., Neil, A. L., Memish, K., Otahal, P., Kilpatrick, M., and Sanderson, K. (2019), 'A systematic review and meta-analysis of workplace mindfulness training randomized controlled trials', *Journal of Occupational Health Psychology*, 24(1), 108.
7. Grossman, P., Niemann, L., Schmidt, S., and Walach, H. (2004), 'Mindfulness-based stress reduction and health benefits: a meta-analysis', *Journal of Psychosomatic Research*, 57(1), 35–43.
8. There's a worksheet on this here: http://compassionfatigue. org/pages/LowImpactDisclosure.pdf
9. Penman, D., and Williams, M. (2011), *Mindfulness: Finding Peace in a Frantic World*, London, Generic.

10 October: Falling Leaves

1. https://www.thegoodgrieftrust.org
2. Kübler-Ross, E. (2008), *On Death and Dying*, London, Routledge.
3. Kübler-Ross, E., and Kessler, D. (2014), *On Grief and Grieving*, London, Simon & Schuster.
4. If you would like to hear a conversation about a digital CBT programme for traumatic grief, I interview Fiona on this podcast who experienced (and recovered from) traumatic grief when her husband died: https://letstalkaboutcbt.libsyn. com/digital-cbt
5. Bisson, J. I. (2007), 'Post-traumatic stress disorder', *British Medical Journal*, 334(7597), 789–93.
6. Haines, S. (2015), *Trauma is Really Strange*, London, Singing Dragon.

11 November: The Joy of Missing Out

1. Westrin, Å., and Lam, R. W. (2007), 'Seasonal affective disorder: a clinical update', *Annals of Clinical Psychiatry*, 19(4), 239–46.

2. For more on the three systems, see Gilbert, P. (2009), 'Introducing compassion-focused therapy', *Advances in Psychiatric Treatment*, 15(3), 199–208.
3. Bonaz, B., Sinniger, V., and Pellissier, S. (2016), 'Anti-inflammatory properties of the vagus nerve: potential therapeutic implications of vagus nerve stimulation', *Journal of Physiology*, 594, 5781–90.
4. Sejnowski, T. J., and Destexhe, A. (2000), 'Why do we sleep?', *Brain Research*, 886(1–2), 208–23.
5. Mignot, E. (2008), 'Why we sleep: the temporal organization of recovery', *PLoS Biology*, 6(4), e106.
6. Espie, C. A. (2006), *Overcoming Insomnia and Sleep Problems: A Self-Help Guide Using Cognitive Behavioural Techniques*, London, Robinson. This is a good book if you have trouble sleeping.

12 December: It's Christmas

1. http://news.bbc.co.uk/1/hi/6197921.stm
2. Baudinet, J., Eisler, I., Dawson, L., Simic, M., and Schmidt, U. (2021), 'Multi-family therapy for eating disorders: a systematic scoping review of the quantitative and qualitative findings', *International Journal of Eating Disorders*, 54(12), 2095–120.
3. Mutz, M. (2016), 'Christmas and subjective well-being: a research note', *Applied Research in Quality of Life*, 11(4), 1341–56.
4. Taylor, L. M., Oldershaw, A., Richards, C., Davidson, K., Schmidt, U., and Simic, M. (2011), 'Development and pilot evaluation of a manualized cognitive-behavioural treatment package for adolescent self-harm', *Behavioural and Cognitive Psychotherapy*, 39(5), 619–25.
5. Rollnick, S., and Miller, W. R. (1995), 'What is motivational interviewing?', *Behavioural and Cognitive Psychotherapy*, 23(4), 325–34.

6. Selekman, M. D. (2006), *Working with Self-Harming Adolescents: A Collaborative, Strengths-Based Therapy Approach*, New York, W. W. Norton & Co.

Epilogue

1. https://www.nice.org.uk/guidance

Index